EASTER
in My HEART

EASTER in My HEART

Uplifting Stories of Redemption & Hope

Compiled & Edited by
Joe Wheeler

WATERBROOK
PRESS

EASTER IN MY HEART
PUBLISHED BY WATERBROOK PRESS
5446 North Academy Boulevard, Suite 200
Colorado Springs, Colorado 80918
A division of Random House, Inc.

ISBN 1-57856-268-6

Published in association with the literary agency of Alive Communications, Inc.,
1465 Kelly Johnson Boulevard, Suite 320, Colorado Springs, Colorado 80920.

Library of Congress Cataloging-in-Publication Data
Easter in my heart: uplifting stories of redemption and hope/[compiled and edited by]
Joe Wheeler.—1st ed.
    p. cm.
  Includes bibliographical references.
  ISBN 1-57856-268-6 (hardcover)
  1. Christian fiction, American. 2. Easter stories. I. Wheeler, Joe L., 1936-

PS648.C43 E27 2000
813.008'0334—dc21

                                     99-055260

Printed in the United States of America
2000—First Edition

10 9 8 7 6 5 4 3 2 1

TO
CONNIE PALMER WHEELER

*For forty years now, she has remained at my side,
through good days and bad, joy and sorrow,
success and failure. In an unstable world, she has been,
and remains, a certainty, a constant, a wife who
signed on for the long haul, the entire journey.
In this ministry of stories, she is an equal partner;
thus this is her book too.
Bless her!*

Table of Contents

Contents

Acknowledgments

Introduction: "Rediscovering Easter," by Joseph Leininger Wheeler, copyright © 1999. Printed by permission of the author.

Introduction: "If Easter Be Not True," by Henry H. Barstow, D.D. If anyone knows of the earliest publication date and publisher of this old poem, please relay that information to Joe Wheeler, care of WaterBrook Press.

"What Was in Jeremy's Egg?" by Ida Mae Kempel. Published in *Focus on the Family Magazine,* April 1988. Reprinted by permission of the author.

"The Arbutus Bonnet," by Margaret E. Sangster, Jr. Reprinted by permission of Christian Herald Association, New York.

"The Maid of Emmaus," by Agnes Sligh Turnbull. Published in Turnbull's *Far Above Rubies,* Fleming H. Revell Company, 1926. Reprinted by permission of Fleming H. Revell, a division of Baker Book House, Grand Rapids, Michigan.

"The Hidden Treasure," by Arthur Gordon. Published in Gordon's *The Hidden Treasure,* Fleming H. Revell Company, 1974. Reprinted by permission of the author.

"An Easter Song," by Grace Ethelyn Cody. Published in *The Youth's Companion,* April 13, 1911.

"Mrs. Pepper Passes," by Helen Ward Banks. Published in *The Youth's Companion,* April 5, 1917.

"Only a Piece of Glass." Author unknown. If anyone can provide knowledge of author, earliest publication, and date of this story, please relay this information to Joe Wheeler, care of WaterBrook Press.

"Polly's Easter Service," by Elizabeth Price. Published in *The Youth's Instructor,* April 5, 1921. Text reprinted by permission of Review and Herald Publishing Association, Hagerstown, Maryland.

"The Gift," by Margaret Prescott Montague. Published in Montague's The Gift (New York: E. P. Dutton, 1919).

"Pieces of Silver," by Clarence Budington Kelland. Published in *Harper's Monthly,* April 1913.

"Lilies for Inspiration," by Mabel McKee. Published in *Young People's Weekly,* March 26, 1932. Reprinted by permission of David C. Cook, Colorado Springs, Colorado; and Fleming H. Revell, a division of Baker Book House, Grand Rapids, Michigan.

"A Glimpse of Heaven," by Harriet Lummis Smith. Published in *Young People's Weekly,* March 26, 1932. Text reprinted by permission of David C. Cook, Colorado Springs, Colorado.

"The Hollow Man," by Joseph Leininger Wheeler, copyright © 1999. Printed by permission of the author.

Woodcut illustrations are from the library of Joe Wheeler.

Rediscovering Easter

Let every man and woman count themselves immortal. Let him catch the revelation of Jesus in His Resurrection. Let him say not merely, "Christ is risen," but "I shall rise.... In me there is something that no stain on earth can tarnish and no stroke of the world can erase. I, too, am a part of God and have God's immortality in me."

—PHILLIPS BROOKS (1835–1893)

The Son of God, coequal with the Father and the Holy Spirit, was dead. Nothing comparable had ever occurred in all the billions of whirling universes created by God. Not even Lucifer's war with his Creator and expulsion from heaven could compare, for the Trinity had been victorious over the forces of evil in that epic struggle.

1

Now, Lucifer had had his way and compelled his minions to slay the Son of God. At that moment, all other action stopped as angels and created beings in other worlds peered down from their far-flung ramparts at this unbelievable event that had taken place on this pinpoint of a planet called earth. Would Lucifer triumph over the Trinity after all? Was the Trinity to be reduced to two?

Even Christ, knowing the end from the beginning, weakened under the battering of Crucifixion Week, and He asked His Father whether it was really necessary for Him to drink the cup of death (Matthew 26:39,42; Mark 14:35-36; Luke 22:42). Worst of all, for the first time in all eternity, God the Father withdrew His presence and protecting hand from His Son, for had He not, Christ never could have validated the contract of our salvation by His death. In the pitch-darkness of the Father's withdrawal could be heard perhaps the most heartbreaking wail in all history: "My God, my God, why have you forsaken me?" (Matthew 27:46; Mark 15:34). As Christ surrendered His Spirit to the Father and died, the earth was shrouded in stygian darkness. Earthquakes convulsed the earth, and lightning and thunder so blinded and deafened the spectators that thousands feared the world was coming to its end. In the midst of it all, many of the saints were resurrected. When the darkness finally receded, there they were, walking the streets of Jerusalem. The Roman officers who had experienced it all had only one answer for these astounding events: "Truly, this was the Son of God!" (Matthew 27:54).

In the Temple, the great curtain separating the Holy from the Most Holy Place was rent by a giant unseen hand, from top to bottom, signifying that further sacrifices were no longer needed: The ultimate sacrifice had been made so that the human race might once again regain eternal life.

But would Christ?

The answer came early that Sunday morning—not all the forces of hell could have kept that great boulder from being rolled aside, nor God the Son from being resurrected.

We have become so accustomed to telling the story, to hearing it and reading it, that we forget how different the world would be had Christ failed to rise from the dead. Had Lucifer triumphed, life would be but a cruel joke; nothing would have any real meaning or relevance.

But Christ *did* rise, and in so doing made possible the eternal life referred to by Phillips Brooks (author of "O Little Town of Bethlehem") in our opening quotation. And all this we remember every Easter.

Or should.

THE PAULINE LEGACY

If Easter be not true,
Then all the lilies low must lie;
The Flanders poppies fade and die.
The spring must lose her fairest bloom,
For Christ were still within the tomb...
If Easter be not true.

If Easter be not true
Then faith must mount on broken wing;
Then hope no more immortal spring.
Then hope must lose her mighty urge;
Life prove a phantom, death a dirge...
If Easter be not true.

If Easter be not true,
'Twere foolishness the cross to bear;
He died in vain who suffered there.
What matter though we laugh or cry,
Be good or evil, live or die,
If Easter be not true?

If Easter be not true...
But it is true, and Christ is risen!

4

And mortal spirit from its prison
Of sin and death with Him may rise!
Worthwhile the struggle, sure the prize,
Since Easter, aye, is true!

—"IF EASTER BE NOT TRUE"
BY HENRY H. BARSTOW, D.D.

For any who yet doubt the truth of the Easter story, all they need to do is to study the life, ministry, philosophy, theology, and writings of one of the greatest minds of all time: Saul of Tarsus. Saul, a Roman citizen, was well educated in Roman, Hellenistic, and Semitic cultures as well as being considered one of the spiritual giants who studied under the legendary Gamaliel in Jerusalem. There are remarkable parallels between the Saul-into-Paul story and that of Martin Luther. Early on, both men were extreme legalists, firmly believing in salvation by perfect observation of the Law. The early lives of both were dominated by their perception of the Law as the defining standard of one's relative goodness or wickedness. It was because Saul believed so completely in Jewish law that he was filled with such hatred against the early Christians. He felt it was blasphemous to replace that Law with a perceived Messiah. He did more than verbally oppose Christian ideals: As a member of the Sanhedrin and the Jewish high command, he was the chief persecutor of the Palestinian Christians. In fact, he had much to do with the stoning of that first Christian martyr, Stephen. Stephen, one of the Seven Deacons, learned in both the Greek and Jewish cultures, was the most eloquent and persuasive of all the early Christian leaders. In his masterful oration of self-defense delivered to the Sanhedrin, Stephen recalled Moses' prophecies regarding the Messiah and declared Christ to be their fulfillment. He appealed to his listeners to see Christ as having redefined the way to eternal life. It was in vain: The Jewish leaders sentenced him to be stoned.

Saul could erase neither Stephen's words nor his calm acceptance of death. Nevertheless, he determined to press on with his bloody sword. On the road to Damascus Christ came to him in a blinding midday encounter. In the darkness that followed, Saul became Paul, second only to Christ in Christian history and thought. The reality of this meeting with his ascended Lord cannot be questioned. Over time, Paul compared what he had seen, heard, and experienced with the apostles who had interacted personally with Christ during His earthly ministry. Paul found no cracks, no discrepancies: Truly, he had communed with the Son of God. He had little to gain and much to lose by this sudden apostasy from Judaism. To contemporaries, his sudden 180-degree turn must have bordered on the inexplicable!

Paul saved early Christianity from degenerating into merely another Jewish sect, from spiraling downward into bondage and religious legalism. In Paul's conversion, Jesus the Christ became as central to his new walk as the Law had been in his old. In this respect, Paul went far beyond the other early church leaders, for he boldly proclaimed that Christ's death on the cross had changed everything, redefined everything. In fact, Paul declared, Christ replaced the Law with Himself and became the medium of communication between God and man. To Paul, Christ was all-in-all, *everything*, and His death and resurrection formed the basis of a totally new way of living, acting, and worshiping. He pointed out that if righteousness resulted merely from observance of the Law, then why did Christ have to die? The Cross was central to Paul, and the majesty of it permeates his writings to the early church, a church he transformed from a Jewish sect into a worldwide fellowship of believers from all nations and races. He wrote not as a theologian, but as a pastor, a prophet, a counselor, a teacher, a mentor, and a missionary, seeking to make the miracle of Christ's death, resurrection, and ascension real and meaningful to each culture. Hence he addressed each group of believers uniquely.

Paul redefined spirituality in moral terms, borrowing heavily from Christ's own words, but also explaining their meaning through the prism of his own human weaknesses and frailties. Eternal life, thanks to Christ's sacrifice, was now a given to all who believed. In union with the Redeemer, each believer was now a son, a daughter, of God, and thus "saved." Having established that truth, he went on to develop the thesis that the "Fruits of the Spirit" reveal whether one is a true believer or a false one. He would have agreed with C. S. Lewis that belief and works are like the two blades of a pair of scissors, each being essential to the scissors' purpose.

Paul so changed the course of Christianity that he became its "second founder." H. Weinel maintains that Paul was "Jesus' most genuine disciple, the one who best understood and reproduced His thought." He also reminded believers of Christ's declaration that eternal life was a present rather than a future reality and way of life, and he fully defined grace for the first time.[1]

---

1. This section made possible by the monumental study of the apostle Paul in the 1946 edition of the *Encyclopedia Britannica*, 17:385–394, and the Stephen section, 21:383–384.

This life-transforming power of Christ's death and resurrection is the focus of the stories contained herein, as I will explain in more detail momentarily.

ALLOWING EASTER TO TRANSFORM US

Long ago, the poet Wordsworth issued a warning about letting the world be "too much with us." If he could only see us now! Children watch TV and computer screens four and a half hours a day (representing sixteen hundred hours a year, as compared to a thousand classroom hours). We adults have mistakenly assumed that the computer age would result in increased time for leisure and reflection. Instead, the reverse is true: Surrounded as we are by electronic gadgetry, we can conceivably work every waking hour. Cell phones follow us outside, into the kitchen, bedroom, and bath, into the car, into the restaurant, into the supermarket, and even to the remotest parts of the planet. Laptop computers make work omnipresent. Satellite uplinks and pagers find us even when we do not wish to be found. As a result we are in grave danger of losing both our personal identity and our relationship with God. Gradually, inexorably, the worlds of work and entertainment seek to gain control of our every waking moment, evicting God in the process.

For those who feel drained by this incessant squirrel wheel of nonstop action, Easter offers an opportunity to stop and reflect. We all have time for what we value most. When a loved one dies, we—who had no time to write a letter to, or telephone, or occasionally visit that person—suddenly have all the time in the world. We notify our employer that there has been a death in the family, cancel all other commitments (no matter how important), and spend whatever money it takes to travel to the place where services are being held. And while there, we are likely to express genuine regret over our failure to better communicate our love to that person while he or she was still with us. It's the same with our soul and our relationship with our Lord: We have as much—or as little—time for Him as we determine.

I suggest that as Easter week approaches, we each determine to spend it with God, to turn off the cacophony of the world and enter into a week of quiet serenity, contemplation, and study of God's Word, especially as it relates to His great sacrifice on our behalf at the Cross. Should we do so, I am convinced our society would be a different place in which to live.

In much of the Christian world, for almost two millenniums, the standard Easter greeting was "Christ is risen!" Today, millions content themselves with colorful Easter clothing, Easter eggs, and Easter parades; the Cross and the Lamb have been replaced by floats and rabbits. It is long past time for Christians to desecularize the holiday. There is nothing inherently wrong with colorful clothes, eggs, and parades, but when these things are perceived as valid substitutes for the spiritual services, traditions, symbolism, and meaning that undergird this Holy Week, a signal opportunity to commune with our Savior is lost.

Paul reminds us again and again of the transformational power of the gospel found in the miracle of Easter. Easter, falling at the season of rebirth for all living things, is the perfect time for spiritual renewal as well, for giving God the opportunity to step in and transform us into His daughters and sons.

Furthermore, Easter should be the most joyful—and thankful—day of the year, for it symbolizes our highest, if not ultimate, hope: the promise of life after death. This promise is perhaps best articulated by the apostle John: "For God so loved the world that he gave his only Son, so that everyone who believes in him will not perish but have eternal life" (John 3:16).

MY OWN JOURNEY

Why is there such a wealth of custom in honor of Christmas and such a dearth in honor of Easter? In the Gospels the Resurrection is described more fully than the Incarnation. Then why has later Christian loyalty enshrined the birth of Jesus in many a song and happy custom, and left the rising of Jesus almost bereft of rich tradition? There's a matter for reflection.

—GEORGE A. BUTTRICK[2]

Given the undeniable fact that Easter (Christ's death, resurrection, and ascension) represents the bedrock upon which Christianity and our lives are built, one would expect evidence of that primacy to be everywhere. Alas, they are not. Permit me to share with you a little of my own journey in this respect.

Out of the mists of my childhood I can see (through the camera lens of memory) Easter processions moving down the street—not marching bands, floats, Shriners,

---

2. George A. Buttrick, Madison Avenue Presbyterian Church, New York. From Buttrick's Introduction to Carl A. Glover's book, *The Easter Radiance* (Nashville: Cokesbury Press, 1937).

horse troops, clowns, and beauty queens but rather the reenactment of Christ's sufferings in Jerusalem two thousand years ago. In Latin America, where I was privileged to spend half of my growing-up years, Easter was not just a mere formality or a child's holiday. Rather, it was a spiritual earthquake that would bring the entire city or town to a halt. And the ringing of the cathedral bells, so loud they swallowed up all other sounds—they are part of me still.

It has been way too long since I was part of such a passion-filled Easter. It is said that Christmas and Easter are the two most significant religious holidays we have, but one would never know that by how we respond to them. At least, not to Easter.

I would guess I am somewhat typical in this respect. Over the past fifty years I have become mightily involved with the season of Christmas but only superficially involved with the season of Easter. In 1989 my life was changed by a coed from Columbia Union College who asked me a simple question: "Dr. Wheeler, have you ever thought of writing a Christmas story?" Because of that question, I wrote one, then another, and another. Because of that question, during the intervening years I have helped to give birth to a dozen *Christmas in My Heart* books for Review and Herald, Doubleday, Tyndale House, and Focus on the Family. In the process, Christmas ceased to be merely a short season for me and my wife, Connie. Instead, it became a year-round presence as we plowed through thousands of Christmas stories in our search for those precious few that are Christ-centered, rather than Santa Claus–centered, and that touch the heart.

Once in a while, as the years passed, I'd consider editing a collection of stories having to do with that other great Christian high day, Easter. But I quickly reconsidered when I found that such stories were almost nonexistent— much, much rarer than Christmas stories!

Thus it was that when Dan Rich and his splendid team at WaterBrook asked if I was interested in putting together a collection of Easter stories, I didn't think it was possible. So I temporized, and I tried to get them to accept a watered-down mix of stories having to do with Easter, springtime, turning points, new beginnings, and New Year's themes. Providentially, they held their ground: *No, what we want are Easter stories that incorporate spiritual values.*

I said I'd see what I could do. First I checked Christian bookstores. No such animal: "Easter stories? Never seen such a book! Ought to be a market for them, though."

Time passed, and the deadline for manuscript submission was fast approaching. I began to get worried. Really worried. So I turned it over to the good Lord: "Father," I prayed, "I believe it is Your will that I put together a collection of Easter stories; if that is true, will You *please* help me?" Right after I turned the matter over to Him, things began happening.

I never cease to be amazed by God's incredible choreography. A number of years ago, when *Christmas in My Heart* was in its infancy, a friend of mine, the Reverend Dr. Darrell Richardson, called me up and told me he was in town for a convention and had brought me a present. It turned out to be a large box of old (well over half a century old) inspirational magazines, all filled with stories. As the years passed by, I looked into the box once, picked out a Christmas story or two, then forgot about it.

Now, on deadline for this Easter collection, I found myself on an apparently dead-end street. There were not nearly enough Christ-centered Easter stories to fill a book. Every morning I would again ask God for help. If it was really His will that such a collection be put together, would He please help me find such stories—and *quickly!* One morning, the conviction came: *Find that box of old magazines!* In due time, I found it and then searched through the entire collection. In the process, I found more great Easter stories than I had encountered in the entire course of my life! How incredible, and humbling, to realize that years ago, God knew the day was coming when those stories would be needed—and had them sent to me ahead of time! I no longer believe in coincidence: I have experienced far too many such instances of divine scripting and choreography. But only recently did I find a biblical basis for that assumption (Psalm 139:1-5,15-16), one of the most life-changing passages in all Scripture.

Strange, isn't it, that such an Easter-story shortage should exist. Once upon a time, for a very short time, Christian writers wrote Easter stories for inspirational journals. Then, suddenly, no one wrote any more. Their inexplicable absence is not unique to the story genre, as I learned while searching for Easter poetry and quotations. Apparently, there is an unspoken assumption that people aren't at all interested in such things!

One never-to-be-forgotten day, I took stock of what the Lord had brought to me. Lo and behold, it was, I believe, as powerful a collection of short stories as I've ever been privileged to place between two covers! By now, I clearly realized that He was at work behind the scenes. This was not merely another book—it was a divinely ordained one.

Now, I belatedly faced another problem: *I had never written an Easter story before—was this going to be the first of my anthologies to be published without a story of my own?* As the deadline neared, again I asked God—as I had so many times before—that if it were His will for a story of mine to be included, would He please help bring the right one to my mind? He did, and He continued to bless and guide my pen during the initial seventy-two-hour gestation period. The result is "The Hollow Man."

THIS FIRST COLLECTION

So here it is: one of the few such collections of Christ-centered Easter stories to appear in more than a century. Providentially, I was able to find enough stories to give me the luxury of weeding out all but those I perceived as the most moving.

As I have found true in other anthologies I have put together, the stories represent a broad approach and sampling of subjects, for there is no one best way to teach values. Most of us today resent overt didacticism in stories, preferring to get the message and lesson indirectly. Thus I have deliberately chosen stories in which the authors permitted the story lines to carry the freight rather than bludgeon readers with conclusions that are already obvious.

Some of the greatest names in Judeo-Christian story writing are represented here, a number of them once famous but now, sadly, oft-forgotten within the Christian community: Margaret E. Sangster, Jr., Arthur Gordon,

Agnes Sligh Turnbull, Mabel McKee, Helen Ward Banks, Margaret Prescott Montague, and Harriet Lummis Smith. Most of the others included were once well known to readers of turn-of-the-century Christian magazines. Several are recent and are still writing.

I feel confident you will agree that their voices need to be heard again as we enter a new century and millennium. In this respect, I view it as providential that I was home-schooled by a remarkable woman, my mother, who filled me with the old-timey, Judeo-Christian gut-wrenchers—the kind of story that moves you so deeply that tears are never far away; the kind of story that makes you a better, kinder, more empathetic person as a result of having listened to it or read it; the kind of story that all but died out with the advent of television in the late 1940s. I am convinced that God preordained me to this ministry of such stories by giving me over half a century to collect those I loved most before the summons came to start putting the collections together.

Even now, we are losing them every year as surviving copies of these wonderful inspirational magazines are hauled out to the dump or they disintegrate or darken because of brittle old age. Saving them ought to be the highest of priorities for a Christian community starved for life-changing stories, for—let's face it—they no longer appear in the textbooks our children and youth read. Apparently, most of today's textbook anthologizers are reluctant to include stories that incorporate traditional Judeo-Christian values. The world the textbooks *do* present, however, is all too often dysfunctional and bordering on the amoral. Thus, if today's parents fail to help their children internalize the right kind of values at home, they should not be surprised to discover that the other kind have been internalized away from home.

We do, in a very real sense, grow into our favorite stories—*become* them; that's why Christ never spoke without using stories. We have an inborn distaste for abstractions, but the stories we love ride a Trojan horse into the very heart of us. The stories we love most we *never* forget.

Years ago I learned that great stories refuse to be pigeonholed or classified, for they deal with *all* of life, not just part of it. Each contributes to fleshing out the reader's philosophy of life, especially if the moralizing is low-key rather than overt. That is why great stories reach us in ways and places the writers would never have guessed.

Two of the stories in this collection, "The Maid of Emmaus" and "Pieces of Silver," have settings in Palestine during Easter week and shortly afterward. Such stories are scarce and hard to find. The rest of the stories are Easter in spirit, showing us how Easter can be incorporated into the

very fabric of our lives. It might be a story of a handi-
capped child like Jeremy, whose mind is capable of steering
through all the superficialities and froth of Easter to the
essence of why we observe it. In "The Arbutus Bonnet,"
we see a preacher's daughter who learns to make do with
the little she has, even to the extent of trusting her future
to flowers from God's own hands. In "The Hidden Treasure," a chance encounter after an Easter sunrise at sea
causes Arthur Gordon to consider the probability that
there is continuity in life—even in our Easters. Two of the
stories, "Polly's Easter Service" and "Only a Piece of Glass,"
remind us that although we may consider ourselves of no
more use than a dusty piece of glass or an ugly brown bulb,
both are essential in the Master's grand plan; both may
flower into breathtaking beauty.

Ah, the transforming power of Easter!

In "An Easter Song," it takes an understanding aunt
and a woman doomed to lifelong blindness to show a
bereaved young woman the difference she might make
during Easter and afterward. A much older woman named
Mrs. Pepper also makes a difference one Easter Sunday,
because she was filled with our Lord's selflessness and
empathy. In "The Gift," a renowned minister finds his
own faith dangerously weak one bleak Easter, confounded
by the death of his own son. Then along comes a woman

who does not profess to believe in God, yet still searches for Him and for answers. Both are brought closer to the Cross during the encounter. Then we meet yet another preacher's daughter in "Lilies for Inspiration," who discovers that, most of all, Easter means sacrifice, service for others. In "A Glimpse of Heaven," we learn that everything—be it sorrow, heartbreak, or blindness—has its purpose, that all things make sense when spread out on the tapestry of eternal life, thus providing a new dimension for Easter. In "The Hollow Man," we discover that nothing makes sense without Christ and His Easter sacrifice for us, that giving rather than getting is what life is really about.

CODA

It is my prayer and my hope that this book will prove to be both a joy and a blessing to you. If you know of additional Easter stories with the same emotive power as these, I would deeply appreciate your sending me copies, with information about authorship, date, and place of earliest publication, if known. As I am editing collections of stories in other genres, I welcome stories outside the Easter genre as well.

There is no valid reason why the season of Easter should not again achieve the rank and place it once had among Christian believers. This incredibly rich season of the year—sometimes stretching from January to June—deserves to have its own literature, its own stories. How wonderful it would be if Christian writers would once again begin to write them!

If our responses from you are positive, we will consider another collection of Easter stories at a later date. I look forward to hearing from you, and you may reach me by writing to:

Joe L. Wheeler, Ph.D.
c/o WaterBrook Press
5446 North Academy Boulevard, Suite 200
Colorado Springs, CO 80918

ONE

What Was in Jeremy's Egg?

Ida Mae Kempel

Jeremy was a misfit in class, so his teacher tried to get his parents to take him elsewhere. He was slow, he was twisted, and he made funny noises—surely, he'd be better off somewhere else.

But all that was before the Easter assignment.

Jeremy was born with a twisted body and a slow mind. At the age of twelve he was still in second grade, seemingly unable to learn. His teacher, Doris Miller, often became exasperated with him. He would squirm in his seat, drool, and make grunting noises.

At other times he spoke clearly and distinctly, as if a spot of light had penetrated the darkness of his pain. Most of the time, however, Jeremy irritated his teacher. One day she called his parents and asked them to come to Saint Theresa's for a consultation.

As the Forresters sat quietly in the empty classroom, Doris said to them, "Jeremy really belongs in a special school. It isn't fair to him to be with younger children who don't have learning problems. Why, there is a five-year gap between his age and that of the other students!"

Mrs. Forrester cried softly into a tissue while her husband spoke.

"Miss Miller," he said, "there is no school of that kind nearby. It would be a terrible shock for Jeremy if we had to take him out of this school. We know he really likes it here."

Doris sat for a long time after they left, staring at the snow outside the window. Its coldness seemed to seep into her soul. She wanted to sympathize with the Forresters. After all, their only child had a terminal illness. But it wasn't fair to keep him in her class. She had eighteen other youngsters to teach, and Jeremy was a distraction. Furthermore, he would never learn to read or write. Why waste any more time trying?

As she pondered the situation, guilt washed over her. "Oh, God," she prayed aloud, "here I am complaining

when my problems are nothing compared to that poor family's! Please help me to be more patient with Jeremy!"

From that day on, she tried hard to ignore Jeremy's noises and his blank stares. Then one day, he limped to her desk, dragging his bad leg behind him.

"I love you, Miss Miller," he exclaimed, loud enough for the whole class to hear. The other students snickered, and Doris's face turned red. She stammered, "Wh-why that's very nice, Jeremy. N-now please take your seat."

Spring came, and the children talked excitedly about the coming of Easter. Doris told them the story of Jesus, and then to emphasize the idea of new life, she gave each of the children a large plastic egg. "Now," she said to them, "I want you to take this home and bring it back tomorrow with something inside that shows new life. Do you understand?"

25

"Yes, Miss Miller!" the children responded enthusiastically—all except for Jeremy. He just listened intently; his eyes never left her face. He did not even make his usual noises.

Had he understood what she had said about Jesus' death and resurrection? Did he understand the assignment? Perhaps she should call his parents and explain the project to them.

That evening, Doris's kitchen sink stopped up. She called the landlord and waited an hour for him to come by and unclog it. After that, she had to shop for groceries, iron a blouse, and prepare a vocabulary test for the next day. She completely forgot about phoning Jeremy's parents.

The next morning, nineteen children came to school, laughing and talking as they placed their eggs in the large wicker basket on Miss Miller's desk. After they completed their math lesson, they sat down to open the eggs.

In the first egg, Doris found a flower. "Oh yes, a flower is certainly a sign of new life," she said. "When plants peek through the ground we know that spring is here." A small girl in the first row waved her arm. "That's my egg, Miss Miller," she called out.

The next egg contained a plastic butterfly, which

looked very real. Doris held it up. "We all know that a caterpillar changes and grows into a beautiful butterfly. Yes, that is new life too." Little Judy smiled proudly and said, "Miss Miller, that one is mine!"

Next, Doris found a rock with moss on it. She explained that moss, too, showed life. Billy spoke up from the back of the classroom, "My daddy helped me!" he beamed.

Then Doris opened the fourth egg. She gasped. The egg was empty! *Surely it must be Jeremy's,* she thought. Of course, he had not understood her instructions. If only she had not forgotten to phone his parents! Because she did not want to embarrass him, she quietly set the egg aside and reached for another.

Suddenly Jeremy spoke up, "Miss Miller, aren't you going to talk about my egg?"

Flustered, Doris replied, "But, Jeremy—your egg is empty!"

He looked into her eyes and said softly, "Yes, but Jesus' tomb was empty too!"

Time stopped. When she could speak again, Doris asked him, "Do you know why the tomb was empty?"

"Oh yes!" Jeremy said, "Jesus was killed and put in there. Then His father raised Him up!"

The recess bell rang. While the children excitedly ran out to the schoolyard, Doris cried. The cold inside her melted completely away.

Three months later, Jeremy died. Those who paid their respects at the mortuary were surprised to see nineteen eggs on top of his casket—all of them empty.

TWO

The Arbutus Bonnet

Margaret E. Sangster, Jr.

Eleanor and Robert had been friends long ago—then he had gone away. Now he was coming back after many years, having grown in so many ways: more cultured, more educated by far than she. She, on the other hand, had remained with her minister father in the small little rural town, supported him, encouraged him, and stayed by him.

She was afraid to meet Robert this Easter Sunday.

She wondered, with his surprising letter in her hand, whether he would be disappointed. After all, the gap between sixteen and twenty-six is a great one. It covers more than a space of ten years. It bridges the gap between girlhood and womanhood!

And then, too, they hadn't even been sweethearts. Not really. They had only been friends—friends who had shared a glorious, unforgettable springtime. A springtime that was gay and mirth-filled and wonderful, that took no account of his wealth or of her poverty!

He had come to the village ten years ago, a pale lad of eighteen convalescing from an illness that had interrupted his studies. The great gray stone house, left in the hands of caretakers ever since Eleanor could remember, had been flung open. Hedges were trimmed and fires were lighted upon broad hearths. And she, coming to deliver the weekly basket of eggs, had met him upon the porch. She had worn a red woolen cape, with the hood pulled over her curly mass of hair. And he, laughing down at her from the top step, had said:

"Hello, little girl out of a storybook! Aren't you afraid the wolf will get you?"

And she had laughed back, quite naturally, and had said in the spirit of the nursery tale:

"But what great eyes you have, Grandfather!"

And that had been the beginning of it all.

There were few young people in the village. Indeed, the village itself was scarcely more than a small cluster of houses gathered around the white church in which her father preached. Just as, Eleanor told herself, her mother's baby chickens gathered—for protection—around the old hen. That was why they saw so much of each other, she and the boy. Even though she was the daughter of the poorest family in the village. Even though he was Robert Grant, Jr., a name that breathed magic through the whole country. For Robert Grant, Sr., was many times a millionaire, and the great stone house—left alone after the fun of building it had passed—was only one of the family's dozen such homes.

As for Eleanor—she hadn't much to offer, not in the way of material things. But her education did not suffer too much in comparison with his. Her father had been the glad possessor of a college education. Her mother had been a teacher before she was a minister's wife. And they were able to give their daughter far more than the village school afforded. A love of good verse, an appreciation of sound and color. A polite smattering of French, a groundwork of Latin. Robert Grant found that this village girl had more actual learning than the girls he met in the great cities, debutantes who lived in and by the flame of the generation. And then there were so many things that those other girls would never know—which even he would never have known, save for Eleanor's sure teaching.

Together they found the place where the first arbutus raised its shy, rosy head. Together they sought the trees where the birds were building new nests. Together they followed many a forest stream to the secret spring or the tiny waterfall that was its beginning. Together they watched the sunset paint the world a glorious crimson. Together, of a Sunday, they sat in the pastor's pew and listened to the words of some lovely Psalm joined in the rhythm of some fine old hymn. Together. Together, always, in the lighthearted companionship of youth. And oftentimes Robert Grant sat at the table in Eleanor's home, sharing with her and her parents the simple fare which marked their dinner hour, sharing with them the joyous conversation that was a part of every meal.

"You know," he told them once, "it's very wonderful to sit down like this, together, and just eat and talk. At home—well, we're never together at home. Mother and Dad, they're always out. Sometimes I have breakfast with Dad (Mother has her breakfast in her room). But sometimes a whole month goes by and we aren't together once at dinner!"

Eleanor's mother had smiled into Robert's face.

"Poor boy!" she had murmured.

The fact that he was the heir to millions hadn't mattered—not when Eleanor was sixteen and he was eighteen!

They had been pals—not sweethearts. There had been no question of anything but friendship between them, a boy-and-girl friendship. Until the day when Robert—no longer a pale lad; a ruddy, healthy chap now—had received the telegraphic summons to return to his city home.

"They're going abroad," he told her. "My parents. They're taking me. I'm to be entered in an English school. But"—was there a quiver in his eighteen-year-old voice?—"but, oh, how I'll miss you!"

Eleanor would miss him, too. Of that there was no question. He had been her playfellow—and such a splendid one.

"But we can write each other," she had told him, "and some day you'll be coming back."

The boy's face was flushing with a sudden emotion that the girl could scarcely understand.

"You bet I'll write," he told her, "and I'll come back, too. You'll see!"

And then all at once he had kissed her. Swiftly, awkwardly, spontaneously.

"I'll come back," he had told her again. "You'll see!"

But, through the space of ten years he had not come back to the village. Never at all!

The school in England had grown into a college. Postgraduate work at Oxford followed. Then a special year in Paris…so it had gone. Robert Grant's letters—for, strangely enough, they had really kept up a correspondence—told her the details of those crowded years. At first they were the letters of a lonely boy writing to the only real comrade he had ever known. Later they became the letters of a man of ambition and taste and charm. In between the lines of them Eleanor could read the promise of the personality who, one day, would take his father's place in the great world of finance. That promise made a sort of barrier that the sixteen-year-old girl had failed to recognize, but that the woman of twenty-six could not miss. For the boy had gone on. And she had stayed.

Stayed, always, in the village. A girl whose bright dreams might never be realized. A girl who was held by ties of custom that she could not break.

Her letters told Robert of her mother's death. Of her problems as the daughter of a minister whose salary seemed smaller each year. They told of her Sunday School class, of her garden, of her pets. Of the small happenings of a small place. But she did not tell of the proposal of marriage that the village physician, young and ardent, had blurted out on a moonlit evening. She did not tell of the wealthy young farmer who had gone away, disappointed, from her door. She could not explain to Robert any more than she could explain to her own heart why she had not accepted either of them. Eligible men were few in the place, but still even an eligible man does not always fill the picture frame that surrounds a girl's ideal! And she could scarcely have explained that!

And then, too, the poverty that had never mattered to the young girl was hard upon the young woman. There were bills to be paid out of the minister's meager stipend, for her mother's last illness had been a lingering one, and even the simplest funerals come high! Always when she needed a new coat there were obligations to meet. Always when she needed a new hat there were taxes due upon the tiny place that was her home. Sometimes, with her back against the wall, she wondered why she had turned aside from the young farmer's pleading voice, from the doctor's offer. After all, they would have meant security for her, and for her father's old age. Security in place of romance. But then, many people never even catch a glimpse of romance. Only—well, she couldn't help wondering what she expected of life. For her one kiss had come from the lips of a boy who was set in a place entirely apart from her world.

In fact, he had almost ceased to be a real person by the time his astonishing message came to her.

❧

"We're on our way back to America," he wrote from abroad, "and we are going straight to the village. After all these years, we're coming back! Not for long—to the village, I mean. Although I'm going to stay on, now, on your side of the ocean. It's time Father took me into one of his offices. We'll only be in the village for Easter week. Mother is bringing a crowd for a house party. It will"—did Eleanor detect a note of reticence?—"it will be great to see you!"

Easter week, and a crowd of young people from the wide, outside world! Easter week, when the springtime earth would be beautiful with its new dress of green leaves and flowers. When the guests at the big house would be like a group of gay, plumaged birds. Easter week. And this one question:

Would Robert Grant, coming back with his own crowd of friends—and with his own memories of another springtime—find her too changed to be even interesting? A country woman gowned in clumsy country dress—not a red-riding-hood child from a fairy tale!

All at once Eleanor wished, as she had never wished before, for some pretty things to wear. Oh, it is natural for a woman to want loveliness when spring is on the land! All at once she was wishing that she could have pretty things to wear on Easter Sunday. So that she could—not compete, of course, but at least be in the same group with this boy whom she had known, and his friends. But, Easter or not, a new wardrobe couldn't be managed. Not with that last installment to pay upon the cemetery plot. Not with a grocery bill to be settled. Perhaps, she told herself, she could manage a straight little frock of some wash material. But that was all!

And yet, as she looked into her mirror, Eleanor knew she was far from plain. The mass of curly hair bound demurely around her head was different from the bobbed hair of the time. But it was much more lovely. Her skin had the pink-and-white freshness of apple blossoms, her eyes the clear blue of the April skies. Plain food and regular hours and sunshine—after all, they are the best beauty doctors!

If only there were some way in which she could make the best of the gifts that had been given her. If only, in some way, she might bring back to this boy, grown older, the shining memory of another springtime!

The night of the letter's arrival, as they sat together in the living room, Eleanor spoke shyly to her father.

"The big stone house—it will be opened again, this spring!" she said.

Her father raised eyes that were preoccupied and grave. Eleanor knew the expression. He was planning his sermon.

"The big house?" he questioned vaguely.

Eleanor wondered why she was suddenly so embarrassed.

"Robert Grant—do you remember, he was here ten years ago?" she asked her father. And then, "He and his family are coming back, for Easter week."

The minister was not quite so vague, now.

"I do remember," he told his daughter. "A nice lad, Robert. We must have him for supper one night!'

Eleanor cast a despairing glance at her father. Things had changed in ten years—why couldn't he realize the difference? Robert, once at home at their simple table, would be out of place now. So she thought. But her next remark was apparently irrelevant.

"I wish that I might have a new dress for Easter," she

said wistfully. "Do you think it's possible, Father? And perhaps—a new hat?"

Worriedly the pastor glanced at his daughter. "Eleanor," he said slowly, "I don't just see how I can manage an extra cent for you. I gave all the change I had to the flower committee. They wanted some lilies for the Easter altar."

Eleanor suppressed a sigh. Covered it, in fact, with a smile. "Well," she told her father, "there's my egg money, of course." Like her mother, like many of the women of the village, she purchased her small luxuries with the proceeds of garden and chicken coop! "Perhaps with it I can get together—"

But the worried expression was growing upon her father's kind face. "My dear," he said, "I…I hate to ask it! But…I was wondering if I could borrow your egg money this month. It's—"

Eleanor's pretty face was almost grim. "It's not for yourself, I'll warrant," she answered.

The minister was coughing behind an apologetic hand. "Old Mrs. Grimes," he said slowly, "broke her glasses today. She's helpless without them. And I don't have to tell you, daughter, that she is like the proverbial church mouse. I promised—" He paused. "I promised her two dollars to go toward new ones."

Even the cotton dress of her modest imagining was slipping. Eleanor sighed.

"I have just two dollars!" she told her father. "Oh, well," she laughed, a trifle mirthlessly. "Mrs. Grimes needs her eyes more than I need a new frock!"

❧

Easter Sunday! Eleanor, hustling her father off to church, could not help glancing furtively toward the great house that towered above the rest of the village. She could see smoke pouring out of tall chimneys—that meant preparation! The caretakers were already preparing elaborate food. Or perhaps a city staff of servants…Oh, well—she turned resolutely to the straightening of her own small house—that need not interest her now. She would not be going near the great house of gray stone. Not any more than Robert would be coming to her home.

Carefully she put things in order. Carefully she changed from her gingham apron frock to her Sunday gown. A prim, old-fashioned gown of gray silk cut over from one that her mother had owned. She adjusted the small black hat that came down, like a quaint bonnet, over her curly hair. The bonnet was so plain; if only it had a cluster of fresh flowers to relieve the plainness of it. But then, plainness was to be admired in a minister's daughter.

It was early to start to church. And her mind—filled with memories, equally crowded with disappointment—was too untranquil to receive the sweetness of the sermon that her father would preach. All at once Eleanor was telling herself that she would renew the past, in her own way. And that she, by doing it, would clear her brain of its troublesome thoughts. She would walk to church through a woodland path, one that she and Robert had been wont to walk together ten years ago. She would fill her very heart with the freshness and beauty of the springtime world!

It was a little mossy path that she chose, a path that led, in a roundabout way, to the very church door. Eleanor walked slowly down the path between budding trees, watching the sunlight, pale gold fingers of it, as it slipped between branches. And then she was conscious of a faint fragrance, a fragrance that was the soul of the springtime: the haunting, wistful perfume of arbutus flowers, hiding below the brown of last autumn's leaves.

All at once Eleanor, with a little cry, was kneeling in the path, was brushing away the brown leaves. There they were—the shy, pink blossoms! As lovely as they had been ten years before, when she and a happy boy went seeking them. They had not changed—these flowers—though she and the boy had gone on. Carefully, so as not to injure the brave roots, she broke the tough, brown little stems. Until, in her hands, she held a round, pompom-like cluster of rosy color. Almost like artificial flowers they were—so perfect, so colorful. Suddenly Eleanor was laughing gaily, as the girl of sixteen had laughed. Why, here was the trimming for her hat. The arbutus was her Easter finery. God's own hand had placed the blossoms in her path!

With quick, excited fingers she removed her hat. A twist of the black ribbon band, a pin from the collar of her dress, and the thing was done. There, on one side of the bonnet, bloomed a magic bouquet—making the hat quainter than ever. Quainter, but infinitely prettier. With the aid of the mirror from her homemade gray silk handbag she resettled the hat on her curly hair, flushing with pleasure at the change. For somehow the new green of the leaves, the blush of the flowers, lent her face a new sparkle, a new zest, a splendid youth. Even the gray silk frock was gay and different!

Not far off, across the quiet Sunday fields, the church bell was ringing. After all, what did a smart dress—an elaborate hat—matter when the world was full of beauty for the mere taking? With quickening breath, with a gallant little smile at the corners of her curving mouth, Eleanor started briskly toward the summons of that ringing bell. She came swiftly out of the forest path, across a green, sweet meadow. Swiftly toward the very church door— walking fast, with light, buoyant steps.

And then—then, just at the place where the meadow met the churchyard, she saw him waiting, curiously apart from the people of the village, set apart by his London-made clothes and his walking stick. But curiously one with the youth and sweetness and gladness of the day. As he stepped forward, his eager glance upon her face, she knew that Robert Grant had not changed too much. That he was still the boy she had known.

"I left the others," he told her a shade breathlessly, as his two hands caught at her hands. "We just got in, you see. I came directly to the church, the place where I knew you'd be. Why, you must have known I was coming here now! You've even gathered"—his eyes were upon the black hat—"you've even gathered the flowers we used to pick together. You're"—all at once he was smiling deep into her eyes—"you're just the same! *I was so afraid that you would have changed!*"

Again the church bells were ringing. They cut like a silver song across the romance of the moment. And Eleanor, meeting Robert's eyes, her hands tight in Robert's hands, did not speak. Did not have to.

For his eyes were not the eyes of the boy who had played joyously with her through the whole of a vanished springtime.

They were the eyes of a boy who had kissed her. The boy who had said:

"I'll come back!"

MARGARET E. SANGSTER, JR. *(1894–1981), granddaughter of the equally illustrious Margaret E. Sangster, Sr. (1838–1912) was born in Brooklyn, New York. Editor, scriptwriter, journalist, short-story writer, and novelist, she was one of the best-known and most revered Christian writers in the early twentieth century. Along the way, she served as a correspondent, columnist, and editor for* Christian Herald Magazine *as well as writing books such as* Cross Roads *(1919),* The Island of Faith *(1921),* The Stars Come Close *(1936), and* Singing on the Road *(1936).*

THREE

The Maid of Emmaus

Agnes Sligh Turnbull

It was a hard life for Martha; blows from Jonas were almost a constant. Sometimes it seemed she had little to live for. But then she became a disciple of *The Christ*.

She would bring Him a gift. The best in her power to offer. But then she faced the tragedy of arriving too late— or had she?

Passover week, and a long, hard day at the inn in Emmaus! From early morning Martha had run here and there, carrying water from the spring, bringing sticks, washing the wooden bowls, sweeping under the long, benchlike table around which the guests ate, grinding more wheat and barley in the mill by the back doorway, hurrying faster and faster under the sharp commands from old Sarah and the quick blows from Jonas, Sarah's husband.

Passover week was always busy. First there came the caravans from the north and west. These found it convenient to stop at the inn for refreshment before they began the last hilly climb, which led to Mount Zion itself. Even as the week wore on there were still many travelers, coming singly and in groups, on foot and on donkeys, but going, going, always going toward Jerusalem. When the Sabbath was past they would all begin to come back, and then there would be another busy time at the inn.

But this week, in spite of the hard days and the blows that seemed somehow to grow more numerous as business increased, Martha had moved as if in a happy dream. She had scarcely seen the faces of the strangers as they sat about the table or passed by on the street. She had obeyed endless harsh directions and surly shouts quickly and mechanically, but with a look that was far away. She had heard never a word of the gossip or comment in the long inn room or around the doorway, for she, too, was planning a pilgrimage.

This evening when her work was finished she slipped out to the garden and stood under the gnarled old olive tree to live over again the wonderful hour that had made life—her miserable, abused, unloved life—blossom into a holy devotion that crowded out all else. Only a bare week ago it had happened. She had been sent on a most surprising commission. Every few months Jonas used to climb upon the small donkey that lived in the shed off the inn room and would ride to Jerusalem with a basket of provisions for Sarah's sister, old Anah, who was very poor. It seemed to Martha as if these trips used to come often, but of late they had become fewer and fewer. Jonas had stiff knees and stooped over now as he walked, and even the two-hour journey was too much for him.

So, three days before Passover, after much advice about the road and her errand and dire threats as to what would befall her when she returned if she did not fulfill all the instructions, she started off on the donkey with the baskets of food and wine hanging from the saddle, on her first trip to Jerusalem.

The wonder and importance of it! She had wished as she rode along that the way might never end, for it meant freedom, and forgetfulness of the ills that made up her days. And then Jerusalem! Somewhere back in the hazy and beautiful past before she had mysteriously become a part of the inn, there had been a mother, she remembered, who had taught her sweet songs about it and talked of its great walls and gates and of the beauty of the holy Temple there. Now she was to see it for herself.

The narrow road was often rocky and steep, but the little donkey was surefooted and traveled steadily. At the end of two hours she was in sight of the city on its high hills, with the soft blue-green of the Mount of Olives showing behind it, and further to the east the Mountains of Moab, like towering fortresses of amethyst and sapphire in the late morning sun.

Her road led up the sharp ravine on the western side, through the narrow passes, and at last through the great walls of which her mother had spoken, at the Joppa gate.

Once past the soldiers with their bright trappings and in the city, the strange scenes became a blurred confusion of beggars and shouting merchants, full-robed Pharisees and rabbis, and moving crowds of men and women and children.

After several frightened inquiries, she had found the Street of the Bakers where Anah lived and had given her the food and wine. Then, after she had brought fresh water and ground some meal and told her all the news of the inn, she fed the donkey, ate the bread she had brought for herself, and started off again through the narrow streets, her heart almost bursting with eagerness. She was going to see the Temple!

More timid inquiries here and there, and then at last— the great stone building with its long pillared colonnade and majestic gates came into view. She dismounted from the donkey and with a hand on its bridle made her way reverently toward the sacred spot.

Within a few rods of it a group of people blocked the way. They had been listening, evidently, to a rabbi and were waiting until He should speak again. Scarcely glancing at them, Martha tried with some impatience to skirt the crowd. Then a voice spoke, and, as though it had called her by name, she stopped wonderingly. Over the heads of the people she could hear it:

"A certain man planted a vineyard, and let it forth to husbandmen, and went into a far country."

It seemed to draw her as if a hand had reached out and caught her own. Cautiously she moved around the outer edge of the crowd, coming up at the side, quite near to the speaker. Then she saw His face. Tired it looked, and sad, but oh, the infinite tenderness of it! Martha watched it with starving eyes.

He went on speaking to the people while they quieted to listen. At last he had finished. The slender young man beside Him motioned the crowd away. Reluctantly they went. All but Martha. She was waiting for the voice to speak again, with her hungry eyes on the strange rabbi's face.

Suddenly He turned and saw her standing there, one

arm about the small donkey's neck. His eyes read hers gravely, then He smiled and held out His hand.

"Thou art little Martha," He said.

And at the gentleness of it she found herself at His feet, sobbing out a wordless tale of the loneliness and weariness of her life with old Jonas and Sarah. Then she felt His hands on her head, and a peace and joy indescribable came over her.

"Fear not, little Martha; thou, too, shalt be my disciple."

She raised her eyes.

"Master," she breathed, "what is thy name?"

"I am called Jesus," He said.

"*The Christ,*" finished a fair young man, who still stood close beside Him.

Then she had kissed the blue and white tassels of His robe and come away, forgetting all about the Temple.

The same rocky road, the same harsh Jonas and Sarah at the end of it, the same inn with its hard duties from daylight till dark, but not the same Martha. He, the strange Master, had called her a disciple; His hands had laid tenderly on her head in blessing.

Since then, one thought had gradually risen above all others. She longed to make Him a gift—something to show Him how much she loved Him. At first the idea brought only a sense of helplessness and despair. What had she, Martha of the inn, that she could give? She had lain awake a long time one night, watching the stars and wondering.

Then, as she sat beside the mill in the morning, grinding the wheat and barley, the idea came. She could make Him some little loaves. He had looked hungry and tired. She could take Him some bread. Oh, not the kind she made for use at the inn, but perfect loaves of the finest wheat. And she would go again to Jerusalem as soon as the Passover week was over, and lay them in His hands.

Now, as she stood under the olive tree, her brows knitted in anxious thought, for there were many difficulties in the way and there were but two days left before the Sabbath. She had discovered that over the next hill there lived a man who had a wonderful kind of wheat that made flour as white as snow. But she had learned, too, that only the very rich went there to buy. She brooded hopelessly.

Then suddenly she remembered her one possession from the far past to which her mother had also belonged— a gold chain, which for some reason Sarah had not taken from her. She loved to feel it and watch the shine of the gold, but it could go for the wheat if the man would accept it.

She would do the grinding after sundown on the Sabbath when Jonas and Sarah had gone to the spring to gossip. Then very, very early on the first day of the week she would rise and bake the loaves and slip away on foot before they would miss her. She would not use the donkey, she decided. That belonged to Jonas, and this was not his errand. She could easily walk. It would all mean a frightful beating when she got back, but what did it matter if she had made her gift to the Master?

The next days, strangely enough for Martha, went as she had hoped they would. She had gone with the gold chain, undiscovered, to the man who had the fine wheat. He had looked surprised, then fingered the gold links covetously, and given her what seemed a large sackful. She had returned, still undiscovered, and hidden it in the garden in a broken part of the wall beneath the oleander tree.

The Sabbath came and dragged its burdensome length till sundown. Martha was trembling with eagerness and daring. Now was the time to begin the preparations. Jonas and Sarah left for the spring, where the old folks gathered in the evenings. Martha watched them out of sight, then worked feverishly. She took the sack from its hiding place and seated herself with it at the mill, a shallow pot beside her to receive the flour.

She poured a few of the precious grains down the hole in the middle of the upper millstone, then ground slowly until the mill was thoroughly cleaned of the common flour still in it. Then, dusting the edges carefully, she poured more wheat and ground again, and then again and again, slowly, using all her strength upon the handle. The flour was as white as snow. She tested it softly between her thumb and finger. It was finer than any she had ever felt. It was almost worthy!

When it had all been placed in the pot, she hid it carefully under a bushel measure in one corner of the inn room. She inspected the leaven, saved from last week's baking. It still looked fresh and light. Then she went out for wood. She chose each piece with the greatest concern. Sometimes the smoke marred the loaves if the wood was too green. At last everything was done, even to selecting a fresh napkin in which to wrap the loaves and deciding upon the basket in which to carry them.

She went out to the garden and stood with her hands clasped on her breast, watching the Mountains of Moab, clothed in the purple and rose of the evening. Below them lay Jerusalem like a secret thing hushed and hidden. Not a breath stirred the bright green leaves of the oleanders along the garden wall. Not a sound rose from the village. It seemed as if the whole world was still, waiting, dumbly expectant, breathlessly impatient, as she was, for the morrow.

When Jonas and Sarah returned, Martha was already unrolling her pallet. Jonas drew the fastening of the door, and they went on up to the roof-chamber where they slept.

A still, starry darkness crept on. Martha lay watching it through the small, open window. A strange stillness it was, soundless and yet athrob with mysterious anticipation as though angels might be hurrying past, unheard, unseen, but pressing softly, eagerly on toward Jerusalem.

Martha awoke, as she had prayed she might, very early—while it was yet dark. It was the first day of the week. It was her great day. In the twinkling of an eye she had slipped into her clothes, rolled up and put away her pallet, and started her work. Into the clean baking trough she poured the snowy flour and mixed with it the salt and water and leaven, leaving it to rise while she built the fire in the oven. She moved softly, taking up and setting down each article with stealthy care. If Jonas or Sarah should wake? The fear was suffocating.

At the end of two hours the mists that had hung over the Mountains of Moab had broken into tiny feathers of cloud against the golden glory that had risen behind them. The mountains gleamed with blue and amber. Over Jerusalem the light of the sunrise seemed to gather and spread as if, perchance, the hurrying angels of the nighttime might now be risen to brood above the city with shining wings.

Martha bent over the small, low oven in an agony of hope and fear, then lifted out the loaves with shaking hands. If there should be one mark, one blemish!

But there was not. In the full light of the doorway she realized with a trembling joy, past belief, that they were perfect. All four of them. White as snow, and light and even.

A stirring came from overhead. She caught up the fresh napkin and spread it in the basket. Upon it she laid the little loaves with exquisite care, folded it over them, and then fled the inn along the street in the direction of the shining light.

When Emmaus was left well behind and she had started up the first long hill, she stopped running and drew a long, shuddering breath of relief. She was safely on her way to the Master. Jonas and Sarah could not stop her now. And here in the basket were her gifts of love.

As she walked on she became aware of a new aliveness in the air about her. Every bird seemed to be singing. The very sky bent down like a warm, sentient thing. And over the steep hillsides, bright masses of anemones, scarlet and white and blue, breathed out the clear, living freshness of the morning as if they had all just been born into bloom. Martha's heart leaped at the beauty of it. Joy gave her strength and lightness of foot. Before she thought it possible she was entering once more the Joppa gate.

Her plan had been quite simple. She would find the Master, doubtless, near the Temple where He had been before. She would wait with the crowd and listen as long as He taught. Then when the others were all gone she would go up to Him and give Him the loaves.

When she came at last in sight of the Temple there were several groups of people in the street. She approached each and scanned it carefully before going on to the next. After patiently searching a second time, the fearful certainty came that He was not there.

She was near the entrance of the Temple now, pausing uncertainly. One of the chief priests was walking back and forth along the corridors. She went close behind him.

"Hast thou seen Jesus, the Christ?" she asked timidly.

The great man started violently. His face was ashy gray. One arm shot threateningly toward her.

"Why askest thou *me?*" he shouted. "Speak not that name to me! *Begone!*"

Martha trembled with dismay as she ran away from the Temple and down the next street. What could the gentle Master have done to anger the priest so?

She continued her search. Everywhere people hurried about their duties; here and there groups excitedly talked. But there was no sign of the rabbi and the young man who had stood beside Him. It was noon and Martha was hungry and tired. She must ask again or she would never find Him.

Two soldiers passed. She feared them, yet respected their power. Perhaps they could help her. She cautiously touched the arm of the one nearest her.

"Dost thou know where the rabbi Jesus is? They call Him the Christ."

The soldier looked at the other and laughed a strange, mirthless laugh. It pierced Martha's heart with a sense of impending doom.

"Hearest thou that?" he said loudly. "She asks us if we know aught of Jesus—we who helped crucify Him the other day."

From Martha's bloodless face her great dark eyes met the soldier's, agonized. He paused and spoke a little more softly:

"Thou hast the truth, child. He was crucified three days ago on Golgotha Hill. Devils they were who ordered it, but so it fell. Thou hast the truth."

They passed on. Martha leaned, sick and fainting, against the wall. *Crucified! Dead!* And in her basket were the little white loaves for Him. And He would never know. His hands would never touch them. The gentle Master, with only love and pity in His face—crucified! And the loaves were white as snow…perfect…to show her love for Him.

At last she roused herself and dragged her way wearily toward the Joppa gate.

A woman was sitting sadly in a doorway. She had a sweet, patient face, and Martha halted, her heart lifting ever so little. One more inquiry; the soldiers might have been mistaken.

"Dost thou know—Jesus?" she asked softly.

For answer the woman's reddened eyes overflowed. She rocked herself to and fro.

"And I trusted," she moaned, "that He was the redeemer of Israel. Some say today that He is alive again, risen, but it is only an idle tale. For I saw Him"—her voice sank to a choking whisper—"I saw Him die."

Martha moved slowly on, the woman rocking and moaning in the doorway.

The afternoon sun was hot now, and Martha's feet were heavy. The deep dust of the road rose to choke and blind her. The sharp stones tripped her and cut her feet. The way back was endless, for now there was no hope. She thought wearily of the freshness and joy of the morning. There would never be such beauty and happiness for her again. She stumbled on—and on.

When she reached the inn, at last, it was late afternoon. She was about to enter the main door when she caught her breath. No, she *could not* surrender the basket to Jonas and Sarah. Better to crush the little loaves in her hands and allow the birds of the air to have them.

She set the basket down beside the eastern door—Sarah rarely went out that way—then went to the front of the inn. With a shout they were both upon her.

"Thou shalt be taught to run away!" old Sarah cried. "Thou shalt be taught to go to Jerusalem without leave! Thou wast seen! It was told us!"

The blows came, as she had known they would. She had no strength to resist. She lay where she had fallen, beside the oven—the oven where only at daybreak she had labored in ecstasy.

At last Jonas snarled: "It is there thou shouldst lie. It is there thou dost belong, under people's feet. But, hearken to this! If any shall come, thou shalt rise up and serve them. The caravans have long since passed, but if there should come a belated traveler rise up and serve him! Or thou shalt receive…"

He was still shaking his great fist as they went out.

Martha lay still. Soon, darkness; but not as of last night, filled with angels. Dead, despairing, empty darkness tonight. She closed her eyes.

All at once there were footsteps along the street. Voices were talking earnestly. She recognized one of them. It was that of Cleopas, the rich vineyard owner. He always stopped at the inn on his trips to and from Jerusalem. A hand opened the door.

"Abide with us," she heard Cleopas say eagerly, "for the day is far spent."

Then they entered: Cleopas and his brother Simon and another—a stranger, whose face was in the shadow.

Martha had risen with infinite pain and now set about placing the food upon the table. She brought the barley cakes and oil, the wine and the raisins, and the meal was ready. Then she stopped. Just outside the eastern door was the basket with its precious offering—the gift of love that could not be bestowed. Here were three men, weary from their journey and hungry.

The struggle in her breast was bitter, but it was brief. She opened the door and lifted the basket. From their napkin she took the four loaves and placed them before the stranger, who sat in the shadows at the head of the table. Her eyes, dim with tears, watched the loaves as they lay there, snowy and fair. The longing love of her heart; the gold chain, her one treasure; her aching limbs; the swelling bruises on her poor beaten body; all these had helped to purchase them. She raised her eyes to the stranger's face, then—a cry!

It was as though all the color of the sunset and the radiance of the morning had united behind it. And out from the shining, majestic and glorified, yet yearning in its compassion and love, *The Face,* but not that of a stranger, appeared.

He was gazing steadfastly upon the little loaves. He touched them, broke them, extended them, and raised His eyes to heaven, while the blinding glory increased.

Cleopas and Simon were leaning forward, breathless, transfixed. Martha had crept closer and knelt within the circle of light.

"Master," she tried to whisper. "Master…"

He turned and looked upon her. No need to speak that which was upon her heart. He knew. He understood.

Gently the radiance enfolded her. Upon her shone the beneficent smile, fraught with heavenly benediction and healing for all earth's wounds.

Then, as softly as the sunset had gone, the celestial light died away. The Master's chair was empty.

Cleopas and Simon sat spellbound, gazing at the place where the splendor had been. Martha still knelt in a rapture of joy and peace.

On the table lay the little white loaves, uneaten, but received and blessed.

AGNES SLIGH TURNBULL *(1888–1958), author of bestsellers such as* The Bishop's Mantle *(1947),* The Gown of Glory *(1952), and* The Golden Journey *(1955), wrote of a world in which values were crucial. Critics might accuse her of lacking realism, but she always maintained that her books and stories mirrored the gentler world she grew up in—a world she felt had much to teach us in our frantic-paced society.*

FOUR

The Hidden Treasure

Arthur Gordon

Easter morning at sea—could anything be more impressive? Few of us have ever experienced it. Arthur Gordon did a number of years ago and has never been able to forget it. But to the old Scotsman he met then, the ocean sunrise service held something more than a beautiful feeling—it held a treasure.

For millions of people on this troubled planet, the year's most poignant moment is dawn on Easter Sunday. It's easy to see why this should be so. Man's deepest dread is the fear of extinction, of being blown out like a candle, of ceasing to be. But on Easter morning, as sunrise leaps across oceans and plains and mountains, Christians everywhere feel a mighty surge of hope in their hearts and are comforted.

All of us have special Easters to look back on. Once, on an ocean liner, I attended a sunrise service. I can see it all still: the first spears of light in the east, the wake arrowing away into the dark, the ageless words of the ageless story.

Afterward the other passengers drifted away, and I found myself at the rail with the chief engineer. He was an old Scotsman, practical and blunt, but with a streak of poetry in him. We had become good friends, as sometimes happens on a sea voyage. The horizon was empty; our ship was alone. But the service had left me with a strange, exhilarating sense of companionship—of having been part of something unseen but very powerful. When I mentioned this, the old Scot did not seem surprised.

"Aye," he said, "what you felt was the treasure, no doubt." And as the dawn raced over us, he went on to explain what he meant.

It was a bit fanciful he admitted, and he could not remember where the idea came from—far back in his childhood, perhaps from his old Gaelic nurse—the idea that ever since the first Easter a vast treasure had been accumulating. Not gold, not silver, not anything like that. No, he said, in this invisible treasure house were stored all

the thoughts, all the emotions that Easter had evoked in countless minds and hearts down through the centuries. All the reverence, the awe and wonder, the love and yearning, the gratitude and prayers.

These things, he said, did not just happen and vanish.

Like particles of energy, they had their own permanence; none was ever lost. They were all still *there*—out of sight, certainly; out of time, perhaps—but with an unending reality of their own, a kind of infinite reservoir that could be sensed and drawn upon by human beings.

"And that," he concluded matter-of-factly, knocking out his pipe against the railing, "is what you were feeling just now: the hidden treasure of Easter."

A fanciful thought, indeed, coming from a man who lived and worked with machinery. But after all, is the idea really so farfetched? We're conditioned to think of reality in terms of tangibles; it's true. But deep within us we know that we are not just nerve and sinew, blood and bone, or even the whirling electrons that underlie and sustain such illusions. We are sometimes more. We are hopes and dreams. We are the great paired opposites: joy and pain, anger and tenderness, tears and laughter. Surely, weighed in the ultimate scale, such things count as much as the measurables that surround us.

In any case, I like to think that the old Scotsman was right—that in the legacies of past Easters there is faith to be borrowed, strength to be sought, courage to be found. Each of us has his problems, his areas of weakness, his moments of despair. But still the triumphant cry comes ringing through the ages: *Be of good cheer; I have overcome the world.*

And it will come again this year, when light pours over the rim of the world and once more it is Easter Day.

ARTHUR GORDON *(1912–) still lives and writes from his natal seacoast near Savannah, Georgia. During his long and memorable career, he edited such renowned magazines as* Good Housekeeping, Cosmopolitan, *and* Guideposts. *He is the author of a number of books, including* Reprisal *(1950),* Norman Vincent Peale: Minister to Millions *(1958),* A Touch of Wonder *(1983), and* Return to Wonder *(1996), as well as several hundred short stories.*

FIVE

An Easter Song

Grace Ethelyn Cody

Gretta just didn't see how she could possibly sing for the Easter service, as her father had asked her. Not *this* Easter, so soon after Mother's passing.

But in her haze of anguish and self-pity, she had forgotten she was not alone in all this, that there were others; for instance, old Mrs. Meredith, now blind. And what about poor Father?

In the doorway Kenneth Barnes paused to look back at Gretta. Perhaps he expected a farewell glance, but the black-gowned girl at the library desk did not stir. For a minute he watched her in silence as she sat there, pen in hand, gazing dully out of the window. "By the way, sister,"

he said at last in a tone of determined cheerfulness, "it's past the time when Mother always brought her amaryllis up from the basement. Shan't I carry it up for you?"

Gretta started. "How did you know I was thinking about that?" she asked.

"I didn't know it."

"Then whatever made you speak of it?"

At first her brother hesitated. Then he came over to the desk and sat down. "I've been thinking about it myself, Gretta," he said. "I'll tell you. I saw that Bridget had gone to tending it down there in the sunny basement window."

Gretta nodded. She had noticed too.

"I guess she thought it might hurt us—make us remember too much—to have it upstairs," Kenneth went on softly, "yet she wanted to take care of it and make it blossom, because Mother always did. And—well, the thing I can't forget is that last year, when Mother asked me to carry the big, heavy thing upstairs for her, I said I was in too much of a hurry and went off downtown and"—the boy's voice choked—"she brought it up herself."

For answer, Gretta suddenly buried her face in her arms on the desk and began to sob bitterly.

"Don't, Gretta, don't—dear!" he begged. "It doesn't do any good."

"Oh, I can't help it!" she cried, passionately. "You

haven't anything to be sorry for, compared with me, Ken! Everyone knows how good you are. But I came home from school that same day, and she was so tired, and I never even noticed the cover she had been putting on the amaryllis jar, or anything like that. I just said the plant was a straggling, overgrown old thing, and I wished we could have some decent houseplants like other people, and oh, I was horrid—horrid! I can see her face now with that hurt look, and I can't bear it, Ken—I can't! If I could only go back and begin over—but she's gone! I've lost my chance! Oh, I wish I could die!"

"Hush, Gretta! Father'll hear."

"I can't help it. I can't always keep it in. I try and try! I was just sitting here, wondering if Father would like to have me put that plant in the bay window, the way Mother always did, and thinking that I couldn't bear to have it here, reminding me every day how I'd lost my chance. Oh, I was always thinking about myself instead of about her, when she was here, and I never even knew it until she was gone!"

Kenneth patted her shoulder and wondered what he could answer.

"I'm pretty sure Father would like it," he said, presently, in a tone of decision. "I'm going straight down to bring it up now."

He was gone before she could object, and when he reappeared with the heavy jar in his arms, Gretta hastily wiped her eyes and cleared the little stand in the window.

"There goes Father to the post office!" exclaimed Kenneth, hearing the front door close. "He likes to have me walk down with him, so I'll run and catch up. You put some kind of a cover 'round the old jar, and take care of it, won't you, Gretta? He'll be pleased if you do."

"I'll try, Ken," she said, brokenly, but the tears had come again, and she could only shake her head, without a word, when Kenneth said, "Don't cry any more now. Brace up. We must, for Father, you know."

❧

Mr. Barnes was shut into his study until late that afternoon. He was writing his Easter sermon, and when at last he came out, there was the shining look of victory after struggle on his pale, worn face. The first words he spoke were, "Mother's amaryllis! That's your work, I know, daughter."

"No; Ken did it," said Gretta, hardly looking up from the stocking she was darning, because she wished to hide the tears that stood in her eyes. She was a pathetic little figure as she sat there with her face bowed over her work, and her father felt it. He crossed the room and laid a tender hand on the yellow braids wound 'round her head.

"Ken may have brought it upstairs," he said, "but 'twas Gretta who put the pretty cover on it, I'm sure. And it's well started already, isn't it? Look at those buds! I believe it will blossom before Easter day!"

Gretta could not answer, but Father understood and, drawing up a chair, he went on with a brave attempt at brightness:

"There's good news for us all tonight. Aunt Elsie writes that she can get away, at last. She'll be here a week from Saturday, the day before Easter, and she'll stay as long as we need her. Aren't we thankful?"

Aunt Elsie was Mr. Barnes's youngest sister, dearly loved by him and both his children, but Gretta could not echo the brightness in his tone. She could only falter, still with downcast eyes. "I suppose we are, Father—as thankful as we can be for anything now."

Then Kenneth came in, and Bridget called the lonely trio to dinner, and at last one more of the hard days came to an end.

They were so long—those days! There was no special

hope in Aunt Elsie's coming, because there was no special hope in anything any more, and yet it seemed months to Gretta before ten days dragged away.

"My precious!" That was all Aunt Elsie said when Gretta met her at the door the morning before Easter, but the little figure in the black dress was clasped close, and Gretta suddenly found comfort.

Then the study door opened behind them. "Stephen—dear, *dear* boy!" cried Aunt Elsie to the Reverend Mr. Barnes, and with one arm still round Gretta, she put the other about her brother's neck. "And Kenneth, too! Another dear boy!" she added a minute later as the tall fellow caught his aunt in a boy's loving hug. That was all. In a few minutes it was as if she had always been there, except for the sudden hint of warmth and brightness through the lonely house.

The greetings were scarcely over before someone called to consult with Mr. Barnes, and he came back to the group with a troubled expression on his face.

"Miss Holbrook has taken ill suddenly," he said. "They have tried everywhere to find someone to sing the solo in her place tomorrow, but there seems to be no one who can do it. Daughter," he added, with a new thought, "I've been planning that the service tomorrow should be for Mama, specially. Not that others should know about it, of course, but I have been thinking about her beautiful life all the time I was writing my sermon, and I wanted it all to be just as she would like it. For the solo I was going to have that little Easter song that she used to love to hear you sing. Could you…do you suppose you could sing it for me?"

Gretta shrank back. "O Father!" she said. She felt two pairs of appealing eyes, Kenneth's and Aunt Elsie's, but neither of them knew what this meant to her. "Father— you couldn't expect—oh, I can't sing! It's gone out of me. I never, never can sing anymore! Don't you know that?"

With the question she was sobbing in his arms—great, racking sobs, such as it hurts the heart to hear—while he patted and soothed her gently.

"There, daughter, I shouldn't have asked it! It was self-ish of me. I had a sudden thought that it would help me so much—give me more strength to go through it all—and I spoke before I thought. I know you can't."

He was no sooner out of the house than Aunt Elsie turned to Gretta with tears welling in her eyes.

"He breaks my heart, Gretta!" she cried. "To see him so thoughtful of others while he's missing her so at every turn himself! When he stood there brushing his own coat collar, it came over me how she always watched for the chance to do those little things for him, and I could hardly bear it."

"But I've tried to do all I could to take care of him, Auntie," protested Gretta, surprised out of her tears. What she had expected was a heart's outpouring of sympathy for herself. "You'll find every one of his buttons sewed on, and his stockings mended, and—"

"Yes, yes, dear, I know, but it's the heart that always thought of him before herself—always, always—don't you know? He's starving without it—and so quiet and brave!" Then, after an instant, she added, in a different tone, "There's her beautiful amaryllis, blossoming away, just as if she were here. I'm glad of its warm brightness for us all. We must keep trying to be bright too, Gretta, for his sake— and for hers."

"But I hate that flower for being red!" said Gretta, bitterly. "It ought to be black this year. How can it be bright?"

Elsie Barnes looked steadily at her niece for a minute or so. "Do you know the story of that amaryllis?" she asked.

"No—or yes; Mother has told me something about it, I think, but it's so long ago that I've forgotten."

"That seems strange. She has had it as long as she has had you, I do believe. Why, you must know Mrs. Meredith, the quaint little lady who gave it to your mother because she was so grateful for your mother's kindness to a little daughter of hers who had died! She was the one who said, 'Mrs. Barnes, I'm going to give you this bulb, and I want you always to remember, when the flower comes out, that it's the blossom of kind deeds.' I suppose the reason I remember it so plainly is because your mother told me the story again when I was here last summer, and she took me out to Bloomingdale with her to see Mrs. Meredith. Don't you remember our going out there, Gretta?"

"Y-yes, I think I do. Wasn't it the day of my class picnic up the river?"

"I believe it was. And I believe you know about Mrs. Meredith, too, don't you—the blind lady who has been out West for ten or twelve years, and who lost her husband, and all her children, and nearly all the money she had, and then lost even her eyesight? There's a brother who supports her, and he wanted her to come and live with his family, but she said she would rather go back to her own little cottage, where she knew her way 'round in the dark, so he pays a woman to look after her there. The day your mother and I went to see her the lilacs were all in bloom, and she was sitting in the doorway smiling to herself because she could enjoy their fragrance even though she couldn't see them. Don't you remember her now?"

"Well, I knew there was a blind Mrs. Meredith, and

that Mother used to go to see her, but she was one of so many that Mother visited! I had forgotten that the amaryllis had anything to do with her."

"Mrs. Meredith wasn't 'one of many.' I should almost think your mother would have taken you out there with her some time."

A look of painful remembrance crossed Gretta's face. "I think she did ask me to go there with her and sing for Mrs. Meredith one day last fall," she confessed, "but I had something else on hand. I was always so taken up with school and my own affairs, I didn't have any time for Mother's plans. I never tried to help her, Aunt Elsie. I was just selfish. That's why I can't bear it now! I can't bear it— I can't!"

Aunt Elsie said nothing, but sat looking at Gretta, waiting for the gust of sorrow to spend itself. She was hoping for something—and it came.

Gretta suddenly lifted her tear-stained face. "I want to go out to Bloomingdale and see Mrs. Meredith this afternoon!" she exclaimed. "Why can't I, Aunt Elsie?"

"No reason in the world. The new trolley-line takes you close to her cottage. And I'll put up a basket of fruit and good things, if you're really going, dear."

"I am going," decided Gretta, with a new look on her listless face.

She found the lilac hedge on each side of the path leading from the gate to the cottage, just as Aunt Elsie had pictured it, except that the blossoms had not come yet. When
she was admitted to the cottage sitting room, she found
the little blind woman, her hands folded on her white
apron. There was an anxious look on her face at the sound
of strange footsteps, but that faded as soon as Gretta spoke
her name.

"Why! It's the singing girl, isn't it?" she asked, searching the doorway with sightless eyes; and then, as Gretta
came close and told her who she was, the old lady gave a
cry of joy.

"Ah! Kneel down by me, dear! Come close," she
begged. "Let me pat your cheeks—they're pink, I know
they are! And your hair—yes, take off the hat, so—your
braids are soft and smooth, just like your mother's! Ah,
child, the world was black to my eyes before, but I could
feel it grow blacker the day I heard that your dear mother
had gone over before me!

"There, dear, your cheeks are wet! I should not have
said that—it hurt you. You see, I'm so used to sitting here
in the dark alone and thinking, thinking about the ones
who are gone, that I don't realize how it seems to the
young. Don't cry, dear! Listen. Did you notice how I asked,
when you came, if you were the singing girl?

"I'm afraid you'll think I'm a queer old woman, but really, you know, there isn't any singing girl at all. She's just a little dream that I comfort myself with, and when I'm alone here, I fancy she comes in and takes me by the hand, and leads me into my parlor there, and puts me in the armchair, and opens the old piano, and sings and sings—just as your mother always did when she came. And do you know, deary, it was because your voice seemed like your mother's, only younger, that I thought for a minute my singing girl had come true? Now do you think I'm a foolish old woman?"

Gretta's tears had stopped falling as she listened to the story of the singing girl, and when it ended, she surprised herself by saying:

"Shall we go into your parlor, Mrs. Meredith, and may I sing to you—for Mother?"

"Oh deary, *could* you?" came the answer in a flutter of delight, and a moment later they were on their way across the room, the weak little old woman leaning for strength on Gretta's arm as they entered the old-fashioned parlor with its gaily flowered velvet carpet, long French windows, and rows of family portraits.

The young girl had a strange feeling that it was some other one, not herself, who opened the lid of the square piano and touched its tinkling keys. It seemed to be another voice, not hers, which rang out sweetly in the dim old room. First she sang some tender little songs of summertime and the outdoors. Then, before she realized that it was coming, she heard from her own lips the melody of the little Easter song that her mother had loved.

Softly the words began:

> If some hand is quite still
> That we have loved and kept in ours until
> It grew so cold;
> If all it held hath fallen from its hold,
> And it can do
> No more, perhaps there are a few
> Small threads that it held fast
> Until the last,
> That we can gather up and weave along
> With patience strong
> In love.
>
> If we bend close to see
> Just what the threads may be
> Which filled the quiet hands,
> Perhaps some strands
> So golden, or so strong, may lie there still
> That we our empty hands may fill

And even yet
Smile though our eyes be wet.

Then came a change in the music, a refrain of Easter gladness, and as Gretta's voice filled the room, she suddenly felt her own heart thrilling with its joy.

A sound made her turn. There, halfway across the floor, stood the little blind woman, with arms outstretched, groping her way toward the singer, and as Gretta sprang to help her, the wavering arms closed 'round her neck, Mrs. Meredith cried:

"O deary, you don't know what you've done for a lonesome old heart! You don't know what you've done! First you sang me roses and lilacs. I could feel them against my face, and smell their sweetness—and *then* you sang me an Easter lily, and I saw it! Child, child—God sent you here!"

And Gretta kissed the old face over and over, as she whispered, "Yes, He sent me. And I'll come again. I'll…I'll be your singing girl!"

When Gretta left the car on her way home, and started up the street to the parsonage, she saw her father a little ahead of her. There was a tired droop about his figure, and for the first time she thought with a pang that he was growing old. Hurrying to catch him, she slipped a hand through his arm.

"Father, I've been out to see Mother's friend Mrs. Meredith this afternoon, and while I was there I found out that I haven't lost my chance—I mean, I can do things for Mother yet. And, Father, I've found out that I *can* sing. I'll sing for you tomorrow, if it will help."

They had reached the parsonage door, and he turned and looked at her searchingly.

"It would be too hard. You would break down."

"No, I'll not break down."

Another straight gaze into her eyes. They met his bravely, and to his unspeakable comfort, he saw them reflecting the clear courage of his own. "Thank you, my child," he said, bending to kiss her. "It will help. The song is part of my sermon."

The next morning in church a slender girl in a white dress stood up among the Easter lilies and sang. It was not a great voice, but sweet, and it went to the hearts of all who heard.

Its spirit of Easter gladness was still glowing in the pastor's face as he came forward and began to speak to his people. Gretta had never heard her father preach like this. Eloquent, tender, courageous, he stood there, the embodiment of a living hope, and his listeners forgot all sorrow in the beautiful inspiration of his message.

The service was over. One by one the friends who had

pressed forward to clasp his hand in thankfulness had gone away, and at last, in the tender hush of the old church, with the fragrance of flowers all about them, the father turned to his child.

"Daughter," he said, "your song gave me strength to speak."

"O Father," she answered, her eyes shining with joy, "not my song! It was Mother's."

SIX

Mrs. Pepper Passes

Helen Ward Banks

Old Mrs. Horn had very little to be happy about in life, and she let the world know of it. The same was true of old Mrs. Pepper, but her message to the world was totally different. On that beautiful Easter morning, oh how Mrs. Pepper wished she could make a difference!

But she was too poor. Or so she thought.

"I ain't going to church," Mrs. Horn declared, "Easter or no Easter! What's the difference of one day from another when every day's as hard as can be for old folks like us?"

But little Mrs. Pepper laughed softly. "Easter's different! Just look out and see! The grass is greening up, and the air's as soft as a baby's hand, and the little white clouds in the blue sky couldn't belong to any other day. Easter's the Resurrection, and everything comes alive again to tell about it."

"It don't tell me nothing about it. If there's a God anywhere, I guess He's forgotten all about any resurrection for old bodies like us. I can't see as Easter helps much. We live on in this Home just the same, and we're going to have corned beef for dinner same as if 'tweren't Easter, and wear our same old clothes. What good does it to us to have the grass green and the sky blue? Might as well be t'other way round for all I care."

"You do make it sound sorter plain," said Mrs. Pepper, with a sigh; but then she brightened. "'Tain't plain, though. It's a world full of love and life and beautiful things, and I'm glad I'm in it, even if I am only an old woman, and no good to anyone. A day like this makes me feel young, like I was going out on adventures."

"I declare, Miz Pepper, I don't believe you ever growed up!" Mrs. Horn exclaimed. "If you don't hurry you'll miss your trolley, and that's all the adventure you'll get."

Mrs. Pepper settled her bonnet and pulled on her gloves. "I'm sorry you won't come, Mrs. Horn; it's a nice trolley ride to Fenton. You won't be lonely, will you? I always like a long quiet morning like this to go back and

remember all the happy things I've had; I never know how many they are till I really sit down to think 'em out. Good-bye!"

Mrs. Pepper got as far as the hall and came back with a bunch of shining daffodils.

"Mrs. Mollin gave them to me," she said, in delight. "Someone sent her a big boxful, and she gave me seven. I'm going to carry them to church, and then I'll bring them back to look at all the week. I'll leave one now to keep you company while I'm gone. Good-bye. I'm real fond of you. I sorter hate to leave you." She bent and kissed her friend's cheek.

"You'll get left yourself if you don't go," said Mrs. Horn grimly. "If you get invited out to dinner, be sure you accept."

Mrs. Pepper laughed at the joke and tripped out of the building. When she had gone, Mrs. Horn grudgingly touched the spot that Mrs. Pepper had kissed and gazed at the gay spring blossom. It reminded her of the row of yellow daffodils that once grew, when she was a little girl in the country, beside the grape arbor.

Mrs. Pepper barely caught her trolley. She paid her first fare out of a purse that held just two quarters, and settled down into her corner.

I'd like to be up on one of those scudding white clouds today, she thought. *Or I'd like to ride in a big, fast automobile like that one going past; but it's a good deal to be thankful for that I've the strength to ride in a trolley and the thirty cents to pay my fare to Fenton and back on an Easter. If I make believe the trolley is an automobile, I can feel just as grand as the women in that one that passed us. I suppose it is silly, but I like to pretend that I'm one of the ones that help the world on. The Lord's got plenty of smart people to do his work. He don't need me, I suppose, but it's something just to be in such a beautiful world and know there is a Resurrection.*

The car, full to its limit, ran through the open country, while Mrs. Pepper smiled happily in her corner and watched the greens of the earth and the blues and the whites of heaven. She smiled at the conductor each time she paid him a nickel, and he relaxed a little the scowl on his brow set there by persons who had not put on their Easter hearts with their Easter hats and who pushed and crowded and scolded. One woman who, to catch the car, had lost her breath used it with increasing volume as she recovered it to let the world know her opinion of the conductor. The man's brow grew blacker as he listened, and it was only by great effort that he kept quiet.

"Please let me off here," Mrs. Pepper said.

As she stepped down she picked a daffodil from her bunch and put it into the conductor's fingers. "I know you have a lot to stand," she whispered, "but it is Easter all the same in spite of folks' tongues."

The man flushed, and his scowl melted into a hearty smile. "Thank you, ma'am," he said. "It's a long time since anyone's given me a flower."

He started the car and, with a tug of new life at his heart, watched Mrs. Pepper's retreating little figure. *She got me just in time,* he thought. *Another minute and I'd have let fly at that woman and then it would have been all up with me—one more complaint at the office and out I'd go.*

Mrs. Pepper trotted down to the big church that she had come so far to attend. She was little and inconspicuous among the crowd in the vestibule, but she stood smiling with childlike content in her blue eyes until someone smiled back and led her to a seat well up toward the front in a pew next to an elegantly dressed woman. Mrs. Pepper smiled at her as she sat down; she recognized her as the woman in the big automobile that had passed the electric car, and she felt as if she had met an old friend.

Mrs. Ashton did not return the greeting, but Mrs. Pepper, not realizing in the least that she had been snubbed, settled herself happily to enjoy the service.

She missed something as it went on. The chancel was wonderfully dressed with flowers, the soft breeze came in through the open windows, the choir sang hallelujahs—but the clergyman's voice was toneless as he read and prayed.

Since Friday he had thrilled with the simplicity and wonder and inspiration of Easter; eagerly he had written his sermon, and eagerly he had prepared his plea for an offering that should provide summer vacations for all the needy mothers and babies in the city. And when he had come to church and looked out over his congregation, the inspiration dropped out of the service. He suddenly shrank from preaching to the worldly, unsympathetic faces before him the sermon that he had written with fast-beating heart. And when he gave his notices he left out entirely the plea for the mothers' vacations.

But as he went into the pulpit for the sermon he looked down into Mrs. Pepper's blue eyes, which were smiling faith and confidence and childlike joy. Straightway in the minister's heart confidence and faith and joy leaped again. He knew that at least one would understand his message.

Mrs. Pepper drank it in breathlessly while the congregation rustled 'round her, shaken by the discovery that they possessed souls.

As the minister ended his sermon he paused and then asked for an Easter offering, for the mothers and babies of the city. The congregation pondered doubtfully—it was a little irregular, but Mrs. Pepper had no doubts. She opened her purse to put her dime into the contribution plate. Mrs. Ashton, looking into the purse, saw the one quarter and the one dime. She saw the fingers fumble for the dime and then close resolutely round the quarter.

They need all I can give, Mrs. Pepper thought, *and I'll walk the last fare; ten cents'll take me 'most home.*

She took out the quarter and closed her purse. Mrs. Ashton understood. With a slight flush she reopened her own mesh bag, thrust back the five-dollar bill that she had taken out and groped down to the bottom for the bill that had "100" printed in its corners. It fell into the plate on top of Mrs. Pepper's quarter.

Mrs. Pepper gasped. "Oh, how wonderful!" she whispered to herself. "Just to think of being able to do that! My quarter won't give half a baby half a day, and hers will keep ten babies five weeks. It does make me most wish I could do something that really counted, but if I can't, I'm glad I can see it done."

Mrs. Ashton's bill preached its way down the aisle until it was covered by fluttering notes of all denominations. The plates were put back into the minister's hands, and his eyes were misty as he spoke the few words of prayer. There was no doubt now about the mothers' vacations.

Mrs. Pepper was waiting for him as he came down from the chancel. "I can't go away without thanking you for that beautiful sermon," she said.

"The sermon *you* preached," he said. "Do you suppose you could spare me one of your daffodils? I'd like to wear it today."

Mrs. Pepper flushed with pleasure, picked out the best and gave it to him before he was swept away by the crowd of his own parishioners. She went down the aisle puzzling over his words.

"How funny! He said the sermon *I* preached!" she exclaimed, laughing to herself. "How mixed up he did get! Now I guess getting through all this crowd I'll miss my trolley."

As she reached the door the electric car was just passing out of sight; the next one would not go for forty minutes. Mrs. Pepper settled herself to patience while the crowd slowly dispersed. At the other side of the vestibule Mrs. Ashton was waiting for her car. Mrs. Pepper smiled at her. This time Mrs. Ashton smiled faintly in return.

"Are you expecting someone?"

"I've missed my trolley; but it's only forty minutes before another comes."

"Forty minutes! That's an age. If you will come with me, we shall probably overtake your trolley. I don't know why Edwards is so late."

"I never rode in an automobile," said Mrs. Pepper, laughing. "It's real good of you. Now I'll get home in time for dinner. Mrs. Horn and me this morning were saying we got a little tired of corned beef for Sunday all the year— even Easter—but when I lost my trolley, corned beef seemed as if it would taste pretty good, after all. You see, at the Home, if we aren't there by one, we miss our dinner."

For twenty minutes Mrs. Pepper chattered on while they waited for the car, and Mrs. Ashton listened with an amused interest. She learned that her guest was Mrs. Pepper, whose roommate was Mrs. Horn. She heard what fun it would be to walk into people's houses and see how they looked, so that you could pretend the Home was furnished like that. She discovered that, if you pretended corned beef was roast duck, it really tasted like it, and that, if Mrs. Pepper were not a person, she should like to be a tree, because its roots were so deep and its head was in the heavens.

Then, just when Mrs. Ashton awoke to the fact that her car was long overdue, it slid round the corner and drew up before the church door. Mrs. Pepper, lingering politely behind, did not hear the cutting words of reproof that fell from Mrs. Ashton's lips. The chauffeur flushed hotly, but Mrs. Ashton gave him no chance to explain his delay.

"I'm afraid we shan't overtake your car now," Mrs. Ashton said, as she put Mrs. Pepper into the automobile, "but I'll take you home."

"Oh, don't!" protested Mrs. Pepper. "It'll be all out of your way. And I ain't a mite hungry. I don't need any dinner on a day when I can ride in an automobile. It's such a wonderful Easter!"

Looking at the little woman who had such great capacity for enjoyment, Mrs. Ashton pondered the difference in their circumstances and their gratitude. A softer feeling stirred her suddenly. She realized that it was again Easter morning as it used to be before life had died for her.

"I'll tell you what we'll do," she said, with a little unexpected laugh. "I'll take you home with me for dinner. I actually am going to have roast duck. I'll telephone the Home and send you back in the afternoon."

"It's a real adventure!" breathed Mrs. Pepper.

"I shall want you at four, Edwards, to take Mrs. Pepper home," Mrs. Ashton said as she left the car.

Edwards touched his cap. He was still smarting under Mrs. Ashton's sharp, unjust words. He had used his best efforts to repair a broken part and had made the delay as short as possible, yet he had received only blame.

Mrs. Pepper followed Mrs. Ashton into the house, where she discovered beauty and luxury that were beyond her fondest dreams. She took it all in with bright, eager eyes; henceforth she should have no difficulty in furnishing her castles in Spain.

The soup and the roast duck and the salad were delicious. Mrs. Pepper laughed softly, and the maid, who was passing her the cheese, looked at her in wonder.

"Things do taste a little better real than when you pretend them," Mrs. Pepper said to her hostess. "I'll have so many new things now to tell stories about I shan't need to use the old ones. Some of the old ones, though, I never get tired of—like my mother. I often play I'm back with her. We were very fond of each other always; it's a comfort remembering you've made people happy, isn't it? I go over and over those days, and I'm sorry for all I didn't do for my mother and glad for all I did. You always are glad—afterwards."

The maid carried away the salad plates, thinking of a letter upstairs full of a mother's pining for a sight of her daughter's face. The girl had meant to have a gay vacation this year and not to go home at all.

When the ice cream was served and Mrs. Pepper had taken a piece of cake, she laid her fork down, with a sober look.

"It makes me think of Mrs. Horn," she said. "I'd clean forgotten her. Here I sit eating all these good things and she with the same old corned beef and bread pudding. Do you think your cook would mind if I didn't eat my cake and took it to Mrs. Horn?"

"She shall have some, and cold duck, too," said Mrs. Ashton, with a laugh, "so you needn't hurt the cook's feelings."

"You're so generous!" sighed Mrs. Pepper. "We don't get rich cake in the Home, and Mrs. Horn has a real sweet tooth. She don't get so much pleasure out of life as I do, for she takes things hard. She frets. The matron does speak out pretty sharp sometimes, but of course she gets tired, having forty old ladies to look after. That's the worst of it—we're all old; if there could only be some children among us!"

She ate her ice cream in silence. They went out to the library for coffee. As Mrs. Pepper took her cup she looked up with an apologetic little laugh.

"It always makes me quiet when I think about children. I love them so! I never had but one of my own—she died when she was seven—but I think about her just as if she were here. Sometimes she's grown up and sometimes she's a baby."

Mrs. Ashton drew a sharp breath. Since her baby had

left her she never had spoken of her, but little Mrs. Pepper would surely understand. She took a photograph from her desk.

"That is my baby," she said softly. "She lived to be five."

"Oh, the darling! The darling!" murmured Mrs. Pepper. Then she glanced 'round the big room. "Houses are empty without children. There ought to be young feet in every home, and young voices."

"It's not fair," Mrs. Ashton said fiercely. "My brother has eight children and no money to bring them up on, and I lose my only one!"

"I used to feel that way," Mrs. Pepper agreed, "but now I'm glad other folks can have 'em if I can't. When I see a pretty little one I make believe it's mine; there's so many children needing mothers and so many mothers needing children—but they wouldn't let me have one at the Home even if I could afford to have it! Best I can do is to keep some peppermints always in my pocket and give one to every child I can. It's in a woman's heart to love children and do all she can for them, isn't it?"

"Would you care to go over the house?" Mrs. Ashton asked abruptly.

"I'd love to," Mrs. Pepper answered, and her happy tongue pattered as fast as her happy feet upstairs and down. "What a place for young folks!" she murmured as she went.

They came back to the library as the clock struck four. Mrs. Ashton rang for the maid to bring Mrs. Pepper's things and went herself to ring for the car.

"Thank you, my dear," Mrs. Pepper said to the girl. "I'd like to give you one of my Easter flowers."

"They're the ones my mother loves best," the maid answered, with a sudden warm surge of love and longing for her mother through her frivolous little heart. "I have a vacation next month and I'm going to see her."

"Could you put me some water in that little vase?" Mrs. Pepper whispered.

She placed the vase before the baby's picture on the desk and set in it one of her yellow daffodils. Then, with the two remaining, she went into the hall where Mrs. Ashton was waiting with a little book in her hand.

"Do you like poetry?" she asked.

"I love it," Mrs. Pepper answered promptly.

"Do you know these lines of Browning's? I've been thinking about them all day:

> "The year's at the spring,
> And day's at the morn;
> Morning's at seven;
> The hill-side's dew-pearled;
> The lark's on the wing;

101

The snail's on the thorn;
God's in His Heaven—
All's right with the world!"

"Ain't it beautiful?" breathed Mrs. Pepper. "Those last two lines I can remember: *'God's in His Heaven—All's right with the world!'* I feel just like that always."

"I'm sure you do," Mrs. Ashton answered. "I see Edwards has the runabout, so you must wear this cloak, and here's Mrs. Horn's box. Someday you must come again and bring her."

"I never can thank you for all you've done for me," Mrs. Pepper faltered. Then, standing on her highest tiptoe, she kissed Margaret Ashton's cheek.

With misty eyes, Mrs. Ashton turned back into the library. On the desk shone the daffodil before the baby's picture. Suddenly the mother dropped into the chair and with her head in her arms shed the tears that start life springing again in a cold heart. Presently she reached for a sheet of paper. She wrote rapidly:

Dear Martin. I need something young in this big
house. Can't you spare me the girl who is longing to
study music and let me educate her? And if she will be

homesick alone, send me too the boy who wants to be
a landscape architect. I'll take good care of them, and
I need them.

—Margaret

Mrs. Pepper, wrapped in Mrs. Ashton's cloak, snuggled
down into her corner and smiled at the chauffeur, but his
young face was reckless and hard. The sting Mrs. Ashton
had planted had rankled into sullenness, and in that mood
he had quarreled with pretty Susie Murphy. Their engage-
ment was broken now, and torn into tatters was the vision
of their home-keeping in Mrs. Ashton's lodge. He would
throw up his position and go west and forget Susie. It was
all ended.

"I'm obliged to you for taking me home," Mrs. Pepper
said. "I hope it isn't using up too much of your time. I'd
like you to have one of my flowers. Hasn't it been a lovely
Easter?"

"I'm glad you think so," he said gruffly. But he picked
up the daffodil, which Mrs. Pepper had laid in the crook of
his arm, and stuck it in his buttonhole. Somehow it made
him think of Susie's bright, laughing face.

"Don't it become you!" Mrs. Pepper exclaimed in
delight. "I shouldn't wonder but there's some girl thinks

you're just about right. You'll be good to her, too; you're that kind. You ain't married?"

"No, nor ever likely to be—now."

Mrs. Pepper laughed shrewdly. "Oh, you young folks! You've been quarreling with her, have you? Well, lovers' quarrels don't count except as excuses for making up. She's crying her eyes out now likely, while you look as glum as an owl. You go home to her and tell her it's Easter and there's only life and love in the world, and you're sorry you forgot it. She'll have her arms 'round your neck before you can say the word. Women are like that."

Edwards looked from the yellow flower in his button-hole to the little lady with the blue eyes. Something hard and heavy in him suddenly turned over and sent bubbling up again all the hope and love and loyalty that were underneath. Yes, women were like that. He straightened at his wheel and laughed. It was easy now to explain the delay of the morning, and in telling his story the last bit of soreness melted.

"Thank you so much," Mrs. Pepper said, as she got down. "It's been such a lovely Easter!"

"And may you have plenty more," Edwards said, as he touched his cap and drove away to Susie as fast as the car could carry him.

Mrs. Pepper pattered up the steps and through the door of the Home. The matron stood in the hall. Mrs. Pepper passed her, smiling, and then turned and went back.

"I had a bunch of Easter daffies this morning," she said. "There's only this one left. I'd like you to have it. We appreciate all you do for us."

The matron's thin lips relaxed, and her eyes looked a little less tired. "I'd almost forgot it was Easter," she said, as she took the flower and went on down to the basement. She had meant to have prunes for supper, but as she sniffed the blossom she decided it might be a good night for the best quince preserves.

Mrs. Pepper cautiously opened her door. She was not sure of Mrs. Horn's mood after being left alone so long.

"Well, you did make a day of it," was Mrs. Horn's welcome.

"And such a day!" exclaimed Mrs. Pepper. "Everyone was so good to me! What do you think I've got for you? Some roast duck and citron cake!"

"Humph!" grunted Mrs. Horn. "You do remember your friends, don't you?"

"Mrs. Ashton sent them to you. She was so good to me. Everyone was. It makes me feel bad to think I'm so useless in such a lovely world. Mrs. Ashton put a hundred dollars in the plate. What do you think of that? I sat right alongside of her and saw her do it."

"Where be all your flowers?" demanded Mrs. Horn. "I thought you was going to bring them home to look at all the week."

"I can look at yours," Mrs. Pepper answered. "One's just as good as a lot."

Mrs. Horn munched a piece of cake. "Good cake. Long time since I tasted any like that. I've been thinking about you today, Miz Pepper. I suppose you won't get a new crown just for cheering up one ugly old woman like me, but at least you did do as much as that. I've been feeling today while I looked at that flower that maybe Easter does mean something. Maybe there's a God somewhere, after all, who cares that there was the Resurrection."

"Flowers are a comfort," Mrs. Pepper answered. "They're like a resurrection themselves—all that beauty coming out of a little black seed. And I'm glad you found out how Easter feels again, Mrs. Horn; it warms you up so. Mrs. Ashton told me some poetry today that was just like Easter. I can remember two lines of it:

> "God's in His Heaven—
> All's right with the world!"

"It sounds pretty!" grunted Mrs. Horn.

"It's real comforting to me," sighed Mrs. Pepper happily, "for it makes me feel that, though God knows I can't do anything to help along, He can take care of things all right, and just spare me room to be happy in."

HELEN WARD BANKS, *born in Brooklyn, New York, late in the nineteenth century, authored such books as* The Boynton Pluck *(1904),* The House of the Lions *(1924), and* The Story of Mexico *(1926).*

SEVEN

Only a Piece of Glass

Author Unknown

What possible difference, one way or another, could a little piece of nondescript glass make? All those other pieces of glass, many of wondrous colors and brilliance—surely the little lost piece of glass would not be missed at all.

Time passed, and the great church window was all but done. But not quite. The Master restlessly searched his studio again and again…looking for that one little piece of insignificant glass.

The studio was far up on the top floor of a great building, and when one entered it, there was little to tell of the greatness of the man who worked there. The floor was littered with bits of glass, putty, and lead. All seemed to be disorder and confusion.

Very early one morning a boy entered the studio bearing in his hands a basket containing bits of glass. Very carefully he laid them on the table, but as he turned, his basket caught a tiny fragment of glass and swept it to the floor. He tried to find it; then the ringing of a bell caused him to leave the room, and the glass was forgotten.

It was only a piece of glass, so what did it matter? It had little beauty, for it was jagged and rough. It was small and lacking in color; so no one noticed it all through the day. It was kicked by the messenger, brushed aside by the maid, and finally, several days later, the piece of glass found itself in a pile of rubbish, ready to be carried to the street.

Now the bit of glass had had dreams of greatness when it had been chosen by the Master. It had dreams of some day being part of a great window in a beautiful church. So as it found itself being pushed farther and farther into the corner it said to itself, *O dear, I had hoped to be of some use somewhere. How dreadful it will be to be thrown out into the street with old bottles and bits of glass. I am sure the Master meant for me some good use, for he was so careful in choosing me. I wonder if there isn't any way by which I can be found? If someone comes this way, I shall prick. If the sunshine comes in the corner, I shall shine. But there seems to be nothing else I can do. I will try, for I don't want to be thrown away.*

So it glistened as best it could, but no one saw. It turned its sharp corners straight, but no one came near.

After some days the Master came to the studio and began to work. He drew aside a homely curtain that was pulled across the rear of the room, and the sunshine streamed through a wonderful window upon which he was working. In the lower part of the window there were many, many little children looking up and smiling. All about them were flowers. Above the children was the figure of a man, as yet incomplete.

With a happy smile, the artist seated himself before the picture. He looked long at the work he had already done. Then he began to put in the pieces of glass he had laid on the table. There was a red piece that finished the robe of the man. Other bits of glass made his hand.

The little bit of glass in the corner heard him talking to himself as he worked. "This is to be my very best," he said. "So many, many months I have worked to make this window. I must tell the world how much I love the Christ. It must be beautiful to show His beauty. If I can only make it express what I feel, how glad I shall be." And he sang as he worked.

The days went by, and as friends stood beside the artist and talked to him, the bit of glass in the corner knew that the window was almost complete. And because it knew this, more and more plainly came the thought, *I was mistaken. There is no place for me in the window; I shall never be missed. I cannot help show the beauty of the Christ to the world. There is no place for me in the plan of the artist.*

Suddenly there was a commotion in the studio. The Master went from one place to another looking for something. The boy was sent for and questioned. Then he was sent to the factory to see if he could find what had been lost. The table was moved; the books were moved; the floor was carefully swept. And the glass heard the artist say: "I can't finish without it. It was such a wonderful piece, and I had spent so much time and thought on it. Where can it be? I just must have it to finish the window. I must have it, I *must.*"

Then the bit of glass in the corner began to dream again: *Can it be I? Could I be an important part of the window? Will the picture be spoiled if I am not there? Did he make me carefully for a special place? Oh, I hope so! I hope someone will find me. All I can do is shine. I will catch the beam of sunshine that is stealing across the floor, and perhaps someone will see me shine.*

So the bit of glass did its best, and the sunshine helped it to sparkle and gleam.

There was a cry of delight, and the bit of glass was pulled from the rubbish pile where it had lain with the other useless things. It was laid in the hand of the Master and turned over and over to see if it had been harmed by its contact with common things. Then it was polished and carried to the window.

A placing of glass, a bit of leading, and lo! The small piece of glass which others had thought useless and not beautiful was the eye of the Christ in the window. The rough places found just their companion pieces, and the color gleamed in the light.

Carefully the artist put it into its place. Eagerly he watched to see what story it would tell. And then he stepped away and looked into the face of the Christ—the eye full of tenderness, love, and compassion. It told to the world the love of the artist for the Christ.

And the bit of glass: Ah! it went out into the world, into the niche of a great and beautiful church. It was one of the smallest and most unattractive bits of glass in the whole window when left by itself; but when used in the way that the Master meant it to be, it became the heart of the window.

To those who looked into the window when they were sad, it brought comfort; to those who were lonely, it brought a message of friendship; to the children it told the love of the Master. To all who looked into the window there came a message of love and beauty.

The bit of glass had found its place—and was content.

FOR SOME UNEXPLAINABLE REASON *this old story by an unknown author moves me deeply. Perhaps because I have known so many people of all ages who belittle themselves because of their perceived plainness or unimportance: What possible role could they have in life? In this season of our Lord's death and resurrection, on our behalf, how appropriate it is for us to recognize that* every *piece of glass is essential; just one missing piece wrecks the stained-glass window. In this season of Easter, when we ponder the transformational power of Christ in our lives, let us remember this story—and what happened when the Master reclaimed what had once been lost!*

EIGHT

Polly's Easter Service

Elizabeth Price

Polly had black eyes and a sharp tongue—so much so that her kind father was somewhat afraid of her. So brash, supercilious, and snippy was she that even the neighbors gave her a wide berth.

Then, her lovely Sunday School teacher gave everyone in her class something ugly that looked like a potato.

Thanks to that "something ugly," Polly's life would never be the same again.

It began in the fall, when Miss Eames brought a bundle to Sunday School—a queer, knobby bundle that the scholars eyed with open curiosity. Was it something to eat? They hoped so.

Miss Eames was a district worker, and her Sunday School met on Front Street, where the city stopped and the big blue bay began. Only very poor people lived there, and the uptown churches never had seemed to find them. But Miss Eames knew them well and spent much time among them, trying to help bodies as well as souls to be clean.

The queer, knobby bundle held an experiment. Miss Eames's own brother had shrieked with laughter at the idea of giving flower bulbs to mission scholars. "They would appreciate onions much more," declared Tom. But the sister had thought the matter over carefully, so she only smiled pleasantly and said, "I'm trying to help them, Tom. I'm praying to help them. I think I'll succeed, and it's worth the effort."

"You're a good little sis—take your onions and go. I won't laugh another giggle," said Tom as he bestowed a spirited hug.

She gave an earnest little talk before she distributed the bulbs, describing the flowers that would reward patient care. "They ought to be in bloom at Easter, children, and you can bring them all back to decorate our room and make things lovely," she finished.

Some of the scholars wriggled, some pouted because the bulbs were not biscuit, and some hummed under their

breath the songs they were impatient to hear. But there was one pair of elfish black eyes that never left Miss Eames's face as she talked, two thin brown hands that clasped each other tightly and did not keep in motion as all the other hands were doing.

These eyes and hands were strangers to the teacher. How Polly Potter ever got into Front Street Mission would have been a mystery to King George's Row, where she lived. They were miles apart—her home and this school— but Polly had a way of turning up in unexpected places, and the dwellers in King George's Row didn't trouble themselves to keep track of her. Her Aunt Millie, who—in a lazy, haphazard sort of way—attempted the guardianship of the motherless little girl, much preferred reading novels to work of any sort, and if Polly didn't interrupt that, she might do pretty much as she pleased. This particular Sunday, she had pleased to walk to the bay side, and had turned into the mission, attracted by the singing. She did not tarry after school to be investigated. There was too much to think about on the way home. So she clasped her bulb tightly and sped away before Miss Eames got to her.

"I don't believe a word of it," she told herself as she walked briskly along. "Of course it's make-believe, but I'm going to try it, just the same. And, Polly Potter, if a real, live white flower comes popping out of this brown—er— potato, then I'm going to get the flower started out of my heart, as she said." She stopped to consider, then began again, "If the one comes true, then the other might, though of course it's make-believe. I'll do the brown potato just like she said, but not a soul's got to know it, only Dad.

Catch me letting those kids laugh when it don't come true! Dad'll get me a flowerpot tomorrow—he won't tell. I can keep it up in my room. Nobody ever goes there but me."

King George's Row wasn't much to look at. Its name was the only imposing part of it. It was only one square long and as wide as the narrow street. Tucked at the foot of a steep hill, it was pretty well hidden from everybody but the people who lived there, and many people in the city had never even heard of it.

A newsboys' boardinghouse was across from Polly's door; Tony, the street piano man, was just above; Hans, who sold sausage sandwiches out of a cart, was just below; and next door lived Pat, the hod carrier. Polly's father was a laborer and worked steadily. He was kind to his only child, but a little afraid of her black eyes and sharp tongue. So the child lived rather a lonely life, in spite of the swarms about her. "Think I'd 'sociate with them?" she demanded of herself, eyeing her neighbors with scorn. "Not so you could notice it." These same neighbors resented her attitude, and if she had not been able to take her own part, she would have been put to rout in daily scoldings. As it was, an understood enmity existed between herself and the rest—especially "those newsies," as she contemptuously called the boarders across the street.

Monday, Dad selected the flowerpot with much

care—a red one with gilt adornings. To his relief, it met with Polly's approval.

"Now don't you tell on me, Dad," she reminded him. "If it happens, it's a surprise, and if it don't, you and I are all that'll know."

"Trust that to me, Polly girl," he answered, pleased at the thought of this secret bond between them.

Up in the little bare room it stood, given what sunshine the tiny window could command and the careful measure of water the teacher had advised. Every morning Polly looked for signs of life, and when the first green blade appeared, she clapped her hands over her mouth to hold back the yell of joy that clamored for utterance. She reported to Miss Eames the next Sunday.

"I didn't believe it," she owned, "but if it comes true, I'm going to do it to my heart—as you said."

"Why, Polly, dear child, that makes me very happy." Miss Eames's arm was close about the erect little figure. "I must come to see you about it."

"No'm, it's too far for you. I'll be here every Sunday till I see if it comes true," and Polly slipped into a seat.

"Tom, help me pray for Polly Potter's bulb," Miss Eames asked that night. "It has begun its mission already."

True to her word, little Polly came regularly to Sunday School. She tucked away in memory's safekeeping every word Miss Eames spoke, to be brought out later if the flower "came true." Slowly but surely, under the gentle instruction, the black eyes softened, the sharp tongue grew more moderate, and Polly waited with increasing patience for the wonder to happen.

The bulb in the red pot developed as if in the most up-to-date hothouse. Polly watched every shining leaf, and when at last a sheaf of buds appeared, her heart almost burst with joy. "It's coming true, I do believe it is! It'll be up to me to do what I said," she reminded herself one day, as she watched the swelling buds, which were turning from pale green to cream. "I've got to think it out so I'll be ready."

Aunt Milly looked up from her book two hours later as Polly came down the creaking stairs. "You been up there all this time?" she asked curiously. "Whatever—"

"I've been busy." That was all Polly answered, and her aunt shook her head. "That's a queer child," she took time to say, then forgot all about it.

The next Sunday Polly said abruptly to Miss Eames, "I'm not going to bring my flower here Easter."

"Why, dear, isn't it doing well?" The teacher's voice was anxious, but her pupil's black eyes sparkled. "It's the prettiest in the world, but I want it at home."

"Very well. I suppose it is too far for you to carry it," began Miss Eames.

Polly shook her head. "It's not that. Dad would bring it. But it's mine, ain't it?"

"Yes, dear, your very own."

"Then I'll keep it. I need it to…to help make the other come true."

"Can you tell me about it?" The teacher's heart was very tender toward this determined little creature.

"Well, I said I'd do it, too, if the flower did, so it's up to me to begin on Easter. King George's Row don't know much about the things you teach us, and I'm going to tell 'em Easter morning, and I need my flower to help."

"Bless your dear heart, you shall have it," Miss Eames promised huskily. That week Polly was quiet and thoughtful. Many times her aunt looked at her curiously, and at last Dad asked, "Ain't sick, are you, Polly girl?"

Polly lifted her head. "I'm busy thinking about my Easter…my Easter meeting."

"Your what?" Aunt Milly let her book fall in her surprise.

"My meeting. I want to ask the newsies and all the rest to come Sunday morning."

"Polly girl, they couldn't get inside," Daddy reminded her gently, while Aunt Milly moaned, "Such a notion! That's what comes of missions and such things."

Polly answered Daddy, "They don't have to come in. They can stand outside anywhere just so they can see what I've got to show."

Daddy lifted his eyebrows inquiringly and nodded toward the stair door. Polly answered with a violent nod and a smile so brilliant it set the man athrill. When had his girl ever looked so happy before? But she laid her finger on her lips. Aunt Milly mustn't know yet. She couldn't run the risk of having the surprise for King George's Row spoiled.

That afternoon she gave her invitations to the newsies and Tony, to Hans and his family, to Pat and his house-hold—to all the dwellers in the teeming row. "You can't all get in at once to see the surprise," she told them. "But you must every one come. Tony, bring your piano, and play something pretty for us."

The newsies were inclined to make fun, but the determination in the snapping eyes kept them quiet. After all, why not? Any diversion would be a change.

"We'll be on hand, but if you're kidding us, Poll, you'd better not." George Grigg looked threatening, but Polly paid no attention—a most remarkable fact.

"Tom, do you happen to know where King George's Row is?" asked Miss Eames at the breakfast table, Easter morning.

"I have that happiness. Are you contemplating a call in that aristocratic neighborhood in the near future?"

"Yes, I am—this morning, if you'll go with me."

"*Today?* Leave our own church after all the extra preparations?" Tom looked his surprise, but his sister only smiled and nodded.

"Yes, just that. I want to follow up the history of one of my bulbs—the one we prayed about, Tom. I think we may not regret missing church for once."

"Very well. I'm ready for anything, so long as you're the instigator," and the young man leaned over to pat a glowing cheek.

Half an hour later they set out on their journey. "It's a glorious morning—almost like early summer. Let's walk," said Tom. "The streetcars don't go very near our destination anyway, and I know a shortcut down the hill. It'll usher us into back-doordom, but I don't suppose anybody'll care 'bout that."

Nobody did. King George's Row was too much engrossed with what was going on in the street itself. "Third house from the end," Miss Eames remembered. "This must be the one, but I suppose we should go to the corner so as to arrive at the front in approved fashion."

Suddenly, the back door flew open and Polly's smiling father stood therein, basin in hand on his way to the hydrant. It didn't take more than a minute for introductions, then her father said, "She's got a roomful of company in there, and a lot on the front stoop; I couldn't even get dressed in time to help her. The crowd got ahead of me." Then he ushered his visitors noiselessly through the kitchen and into the little front room.

There it was in the window, which was open wide—a magnificent, stately Easter lily with a circling crown of waxen blooms. At the window stood Polly, looking out on a crowd of neighbors. The child was talking of her flower: "It's the truth," she declared. "I didn't believe it myself when I brought home the brown, potato-looking thing. But there it is—water and sunshine brought it out, just like my teacher said it would." She paused, but the crowd was still, held by the commanding little figure and the steady eyes. "We're every one of us like the brown thing—every single one," Polly began again, "and long as we stay that way we'll be ugly and horrid. But God can make us different—like He made my flower. You needn't laugh, George Grigg. It's true—my teacher said so and she knows.

And I…I'm going to—" The brave voice shook a little, then went on. "I've been ugly and hateful all my life, and you can't deny it, but I'm tired of it. I'm tired of all of us. Let's get busy and be…be different. I'm going to begin by not being so mean to everybody. I'm going to try to treat you all better, and maybe in my school I'll learn more—" The voice caught and tangled itself in a sob.

Then a kind arm slipped about the little figure in the window and a sweet face appeared over Polly's shoulder. "My friends," said a new voice, "I want to tell you a story." Then, simply, Miss Eames told of the crucified and risen Savior and all He might mean—all He wanted to do for the people in King George's Row. Her lovely, glowing face held the attention of every one. Through it all, Polly stood, her face radiant with joy, and when Miss Eames paused, she cried eagerly, "Play, Tony." It was just an Italian melody that Tony played on his street piano, jangly and somewhat off-key, but somehow it went straight to the hearts of Polly's ill-assorted guests.

When it was finished, Polly said, a little shyly: "You can every one come in and look at my flower. It's going to stay right in that window, long as it lasts, so every time you go past you can see it. And long as it lasts it's going to keep on saying, 'Let's be different.'"

Miss Eames and Tom stayed till the crowd had filed in and out—stayed to drop a word of good cheer here and advice there. Then they stood in the front door and sang together a glad Easter carol for the people outside.

"But it was your service, Polly dear," the teacher said as she bade the family good-bye a little later. "You are the one to help your hope come true. And, Polly, never forget that a life that grows and develops out of the ugly brown bulb of selfishness and unkindness is more beautiful than any lily that ever bloomed."

Polly stood straight and lifted her head with its determined toss. "We've begun, and we're not going to stop till everybody in King George's Row is different, Aunt Milly and Dad and I aren't, Miss Eames. I'm going to ask Jesus to help me not to be cross and sulky and scoldy any more— oh, and just lots and lots of other things."

"You can't fail, Polly," said Miss Eames, softly, "if you trust Him."

NINE

The Gift

Margaret Prescott Montague

The Reverend Thomas McCord had lost everything he really valued in life. But now, he realized in despair, he had lost more even than that—his faith in God!

How, *how* could he possibly preach that Easter sermon tomorrow morning?

Then came to him in his suffering a woman in greater anguish still. A nonbeliever, yet one who yearned to believe; a woman with no hope, yet one who longed for the hope he might perhaps give her. What should he do or say? Should he turn her away without hope? He couldn't, any more than Christ could turn away the thief on the cross who knew nothing of the plan of salvation. All these thoughts swept through the mind of the Reverend McCord as he listened to her sorrowing cries. Could it be God was comforting him even as he comforted her?

Clearly, God had been speaking to her, just as He spoke to the nonbelieving woman at the well in Samaria.

What could he say? What *should* he say?

The two men went slowly down the garden path together: the one rather short and thickset, but light enough in his movements; the other in clerical dress, tall and spare, stooping a little in his walk, his head dropped forward on his chest. At the gate they paused.

"Well, good-bye," the shorter man said heartily, holding out his hand. "Good-bye, old man. It was a real inspiration of mine to stop over between trains and talk my perplexities out with you. You've cleared the whole atmosphere for me. It's wonderful to come into your old friend's garden out of all this welter of a world at war and find him just the same—still believing in God and standing for righteousness. You always did put heart and the fear of the Lord into your friends."

A deeper shade passed over the Reverend Thomas McCord's face, and he turned his eyes hastily away, but his friend, full of his own thoughts, went on unheeding.

"You know," he said, with an embarrassed laugh, "I

wouldn't say this if I didn't know I was just running for my train, but for more of the old crowd than you ever suspect, you stand for a sort of rock of Gibraltar that we anchor on. When we're up against some particular bit of life's devilishness, we say, 'Well, anyhow, there's old Tom—he's still standing firm; he still believes in the eternal verities.' Now I'm off," he ended, with a final handclasp, and turned quickly to go; then, struck for the first time by a gray, stunned look on the other's face, he turned back again, startled.

"But, I say, you don't look very fit yourself," he said. "Here I've been so full of my own difficulties, I never asked how things are going with you. How's young Tom? Doing great things over there, I bet. Goodness, what have I said!"

He broke off, aghast, aware the moment the careless words were out of his mouth that he had uncovered a bottomless pit of grief.

"Tom was killed on the twelfth," the other said in a dead voice. "I heard two weeks ago. I…I knew you hadn't heard, Jim"—he touched his friend's shoulder for an instant with a shaken but forgiving hand—"but I…I couldn't speak of it."

Then he turned and fled with hurrying strides away up the garden path.

The other man looked after him, appalled. "Oh no!

Young Tom killed!" he whispered. "Why, that will be the end of the world for his father!"

But he did not try to follow. He knew that what he had seen on his friend's face was past all consolation he had to offer, and the world was at war, and he was due in Washington. And so, shocked and distressed, he turned and made his way sadly to the station.

As Thomas McCord left his friend and went up the garden path with those long, hurrying strides, a terrible door in his brain opened, and a cry rushed out in a young, horrified voice: "*I'm blind*—I can't see a thing!"

The garden and the path swam before him as he made his way to the little summerhouse and there sat heavily down. It was an early spring after a hard winter, and the climbing roses on the summerhouse were out in full leaf; spring bulbs also were in bloom, and many of the flowering shrubs as well. From his perch on the top of the rectory chimney the mockingbird poured forth a stream of golden joy.

Three weeks ago these would all have been things to write to young Tom about. "You know," the boy had written in one of his letters, "when I have a little breathing space, I run away in my mind from all this filth and awfulness to you and the rectory garden, and we walk about it together and tell the towers thereof! So be sure and write me all about it." But now the boy who had loved it would never see the garden again.

This little secluded summerhouse, the vines of which hid one from the rest of the garden, while its open sides looked out over a steep declivity down on the broad, sunlit valley below, had always been a favorite retreat with Thomas McCord. Here he had dreamed of young Tom's future; here thought out many a sermon; here time and again the Great Companion had seemed to come to him. He would not come now. "I'm blind—I can't see a thing!" His son—all that the reverend had in the world—had died in France, blind and among strangers, and he had not been there to take his boy's hands, to hold them fast, to speak to him of the Light beyond. Was there a good God after all? Had he given his whole life to His service to be taunted so terribly in his old age? And tomorrow was Easter, and he must preach to his people about God's love and promises, about the Everlasting Arms, and "Let not your heart be troubled."

On the little rustic table of the summerhouse, he stretched out his arms and bowed his head upon them. He did not groan. There was no groan deep enough to plumb the depth of his agony. His only child had been snatched from him, and his faith in God was cut from under his feet.

The brief official notice of the boy's death had come two weeks ago. This morning there had followed a letter, with further particulars, from the nurse who had been with him at the end. She had begun her letter very kindly, evidently intent upon giving him all the details. Tom had been unconscious at first, it seemed, but after a little while he had come to.

"I must tell you all for the sake of the end," the letter continued. "He stirred and reached out his hand, and when I took it, he asked, 'Where am I?' I told him. 'Why isn't there any light?' he said; and then in a moment he guessed. 'Oh!' he cried, 'I'm blind—I can't see a thing!'"

Thomas McCord folded the letter hastily here, and put it away. That had been the crashing climax of his grief.

For two weeks the blow of his son's death had gone with him hour by hour, all through the cruel days and the more cruel nights. He had not slept save for brief periods of sheer exhaustion, and then it was always to wake again into the dark nightmare. He had somehow managed to get through the daily Lenten services; he had managed the Good Friday ones of yesterday; but all the time he had had no sense of God to sustain him, and he had felt his old faith slipping and slipping from under him. This morning the climax of his suffering and despair had come with the letter. His boy was gone, and he was in a waste place from which his God had gone also; and with the blankness that was in his heart, how could he go into the pulpit tomorrow and preach of love and faith and Easter promises?

Though Thomas McCord had always tried to be patient and understanding with those whose faith had deserted them, when grief struck at their own hearts, nevertheless, he had always in the back of his mind a secret contempt for such weakness. Yet here he was, now, in the same plight. In vain he tried to reassure himself with the thought that most of this awful blankness was due to physical exhaustion. It was not real unbelief, he told himself; it was only that his grief-stricken, confused mind was too stunned to find its way into that assurance of God which had been his for so long. Thus he had managed to keep himself together through the terrible days, holding on desperately, waiting for the light to return. But today the letter had come, and he found himself in the depths of a black despair, from which all the old sense of an enfolding presence had been swept into nothingness.

In these later years of his life there had come an infinitely wonderful superstructure to the foundation of his old faith. God had seemed to become his very friend. Before his study fire, in his church, working in his garden, and, most often of all, at night just as he dropped off to sleep, he had experienced, again and again, that enfolding sense of the Great Friendship. But now that was all gone, and in the blackness of his thought, he wondered if it could ever have been more than his own imagination, built up out of good health and the happiness of his life with his boy.

And tomorrow, with the big German drive on, and soldiers giving up their lives by the thousands, there was an Easter sermon to be preached to a congregation from which many of its young men had gone over the seas to France, or were very soon to go.

That was the immediate and most terrible part of it all for Thomas McCord. He was very truly a pastor—for years he had suffered with his flock, rejoiced with them, and been their leader, and he knew without any vanity that what his friend had said about people resting on his faith was true. For years his congregation had rested on him; now, at this grim wartime Easter, when they needed him more than ever, he was to fail them. He knew also that much more than Thomas McCord would be weighed in the balance tomorrow and found wanting. If he, who had always proclaimed God so triumphantly to them, could not now, in the face of his own grief, stand up in the pulpit before them and steadfastly reaffirm his faith, then there would be plenty who would not think religion worth bothering with. Tomorrow the church would be filled with flowers and triumphal music; but to complete the picture, to bring home the hope of all these things, their rector, in spite of his son dead in France, must be there in his pulpit with a message of hope and faith for his people.

With his head still buried deep in his arms, he prayed into that blank space within, which heretofore had been filled and overflowing with the presence of God. "Lord and Life-giver," he whispered, "help me, help me!"

He straightened up wearily then, and looked out over the wide stretches of the valley, seeking to rest his aching eyes with its spring effulgence. Below him was the sprawling village, and the prosperous farmlands of his people, with white roads wriggling in every direction. For a time he watched the scattered traffic of these roads, unseeingly. Then, far away on the Winston Pike, he was attracted by a motor car moving very quickly. Drearily he fell to watching it. There was something swift and inexorable in the way it came on, passing team after team of horses and slower cars on the way. To his distorted mind it seemed to visualize the coming of the letter. Nothing had stopped it either; nothing had turned it aside until it found the destination of his heart and stabbed its message home.

Very smoothly and fluidly the car came, winking now and again in the sunlight. If it turned off to the right, it was going to Beckly and not his village. It did not turn, but kept straight on into the village main street. If it kept down the street to the end, then it was bound either for the rectory or for Williams's farm on the left.

He began to dread the thing moving so swiftly and so surely. It must not come to him. This terrible Easter Eve must not bring any more people out of the world's tragedy seeking strength and refuge in his garden. But the car came straight down to the end of the street; at Williams's farm it did not turn, and in a moment more it was rushing up his drive, stopping at his gate.

It was a handsome car, all its appointments speaking of wealth and luxury. Two women got out of it. One was all in gray—long gray cloak, gray veil, and gray sad face. The other, much younger, helped the gray-clad figure to descend, with a certain air of professional solicitude. She would have taken her arm and entered with her, but the gray woman waved her aside, and came through the little gate alone.

Thomas McCord forced himself to rise and go forth to meet this fresh demand.

"Mr. McCord?" she questioned as he came down the path; and at his bow of assent, she went on in a small breathless voice, "May I see you? May I talk to you for a few minutes? I am Mrs. Seldon. I've come from Winston to see you."

"Let us come into the summerhouse; it is pleasant there and we shall not be disturbed," he said.

When they were seated, she went on again, still hesitating a little, still a little breathless.

"I heard you preach once at Winston—in Saint John's Church there. It was soon after Richard—after my son—was killed."

"Your son?" he breathed.

Her face quivered.

"Yes, my only boy," she answered. "He was killed early in the war, more than two years ago. And...and I've come to you," she went on presently, "because, after I heard you preach that day, I knew if anybody could ever help me it would be you. Your faith is so strong—you seemed inspired."

A shudder of revulsion went through him. He remembered that day at Saint John's well. He had seemed to himself inspired then—but now? Yet the habit of service was so strong upon him that she was conscious of no faltering in his manner. She only felt the presence of one who would completely understand, one to whom she might tell her uttermost trouble.

He waited quietly, not looking at her, looking down instead at his own clasped hands. But the few glances he had bestowed upon her had enabled his trained perceptions to build up some idea of her character. She gave him the impression of a small personality, a childishly undeveloped woman, stunted by ease and money, yet under it all there was something else that was poignantly appealing. There was a certain surprising air of courage and steadfastness, the impression of a child facing something terrible, and yet trying desperately hard to be good. He guessed, moreover, that she was very ill.

She had drawn her gray gloves feverishly from her hands, and folded and unfolded them as she talked.

"You see, I'm dying," she began abruptly, "and so I've come to you to hear you say again, as you did that day, that there is a God who cares."

He raised his eyes quickly and would have spoken, but she rushed on unheedingly.

"One does come to clergymen in trouble, doesn't one?" she asked with that pathetic air of an uncertain child.

"Certainly," he forced himself to answer, as he would have answered in the past, "that is what we are here for."

"I thought so, but I wasn't sure. You see, I know so very little about clergymen, or religious things—it's all an uncharted sea to me. I don't seem to have any natural faith, either; I just grope about in the dark."

"Your husband?" he questioned, fencing for time, to put off as long as possible the moment when she would call upon him to declare his faith.

"My husband is always so kind," she answered. "He has given me…he has always given me everything that money could buy."

He did not say the words that trembled on his lips, but she answered his unspoken thought.

"Yes, I know now that that is very little," she assented. "But I used not to think so. It was all I wanted at first—all I really cared about. But since the war—" Again he did not speak, but again she seemed to glimpse his thought. "Yes, the war has put money in its proper place for a lot of us," she said. "It didn't keep my boy from being killed, and it can't keep me from dying a dreadful death. Life is bigger than money." She stated the fact as if it had come to her as a real discovery. "I know that now, but there were a lot in my set who didn't know it before the war."

"Your son—tell me about him," he said gently. He was still fencing for time.

"He wanted to go at once, in 1914. He seemed somehow to see things straight from the very first. But we didn't. We said it wasn't any of our business. My husband said"—but she caught herself up, hastily and loyally, and changed it to—"*we* said—God forgive us!—'Let them kill one another; what do we care? There're too many of them over there anyway.' So he ran away to Canada, and enlisted, and…and was gassed. And I don't know whether he ever got any of our letters. He may have died thinking we were still angry with him. And now," she went on after a moment, "I shall never see him again. I don't believe in survival of the personality—I don't think I do, I never have. But…but," she said stumblingly, "I think if you would help me, I could believe in a God who cared."

Suddenly she began to beg piteously, as if to coax him into giving her the faith she needed. "Please! Oh, please!" she implored, "I want so little. I don't need any of the extra frills of belief. I don't need to believe in heaven or hell, or that I survive—I should like to, but I don't think I can, and that is not necessary. All I need," she reiterated passionately, "is just a God who cares. And you needn't bother about arguments out of books, and dogmas—I shouldn't understand them, they wouldn't convince me. But I thought, if I could just hear you proclaim God once more, and *look* the way you did that day at Saint John's, that would be all I should need. Please, please…"

Her fingers were twisted together and her tragic eyes implored him. He put his steadying hand over hers and made himself speak quietly.

"Try to tell me exactly what you mean," he said.

They were just two tragic souls groping together through the dark.

"Forgive me," she apologized, making an effort to control herself, again with that pathetic suggestion of a child trying to be good. "It's…it's this way," she went on in her hurrying nervous voice. "I know I can't live—I made them tell me—and soon now, very soon, I shall have weeks and weeks and perhaps even months and months of supreme suffering and all that goes with it—despair, disintegration of character. Oh! I know what it will be like! I've had twinges already. The drugs give out after a time—they don't tell me, of course, but I know they do. I knew a man who had…who had this disease, and every day for three weeks he begged the doctor to kill him. And the doctor wouldn't, of course he wouldn't. But I wouldn't leave it to the doctor; I'd do it myself. Why should I suffer so if there is no big plan of things—if there is no God who cares what we do? They couldn't keep me from it. They would leave me alone once too often, or someone would drop asleep when they should have watched, and…and why shouldn't I do it?" she reiterated violently. "Why shouldn't I find release and nothingness if it makes no difference whether we are good or not—if there is no big plan being worked out through humanity? Some people," she went on at a different angle, "would think I was justified in doing it anyway, would think I had a right to put an end to hopeless suffering."

"Would you think so?" he asked, to test her.

"No," she said simply, "I wouldn't. I've always considered suicide wrong, and I always shall. I haven't been much, perhaps, but I've never been a coward. And to wriggle out at the end like that would be cowardly, to my mind, and going against all my moral code."

"Tell me exactly what you need to believe to keep you from this terrible thing, and to help you through your agony," he urged.

She rose like one making a confession of faith, and stood, a gray little figure, looking out across the wide valley beginning now to dim in the late afternoon light.

"I do not need heaven, and I do not fear hell," she said. "But there must be a great plan moving through it all. Life must not be a fantastic chaos, and it must make a difference what we do. Something must be served. There must be some great scheme running through it all, something which we cannot grasp, perhaps, but which we may serve. And there must be a God who cares, who wants our help in this great game. Righteousness and self-sacrifice and courage, and oh, all the little bits of plain everyday goodness must not be wasted: they must be gathered up into a great whole, must become part of something permanent. Oh! oh!" she broke down suddenly, "why do I put it in this cold way? What I *really* need to believe is that what my son did served some great magnificent purpose—not just the immediate one of beating back the enemy—but something beyond even that. That it did make a difference to God, and to His plan, that Dickie—that my boy—should so willingly have offered up his joyous young life for what he thought was right—should have been willing to die so frightfully on the battlefield, instead of living out all the beautiful days that might have been his. I must believe that there is a God who cares for the unspeakably precious gift that my son offered, or else I shall turn my back upon what I consider to be right—I will not serve out my term."

He had risen and was standing beside her; and now the dark barrier within him was beginning to break up, and a luminous emotion was beating in upon him. Yet he still persisted; he had to have it stated in so many words.

"Then," he said, "with, as you say, no fear of hell and no hope of heaven, if you believed that you were taking part in a great plan, directed by God who appreciated the help humanity tried to offer Him, you would be willing to endure these days of agony—some of the torture of which you have already experienced—even though you have no belief in the slightest personal reward for it, and no hope of ever seeing your son again?"

"Yes," she answered simply, and he knew she spoke the absolute truth; "I should be willing to do it then—I should be almost *glad* to do it. I should be walking where my son walked, and serving as he had served."

Her simple declaration swept away the last walls of his despair and doubt, and great waves of illumination surged in upon him. All unconsciously she had rediscovered God for him. She had revealed Him at work in the heart of the race. Her stumbling words had seemed to uncover the very soul of humanity, to reveal all its aching, passionate, heroic desire for service in the great cause of righteousness, no matter at what cost of personal agony. And if this amazing, this transcendent and unselfish thing was there in the depths of humanity, then God was the only thing that could account for it. If a little woman, ordinary enough according to her own confession, could be strengthened to face weeks of extreme suffering by the thought that her loyalty served some great cause, then there must surely be the God he had always trusted and labored for—only He could inspire flesh to such amazing heroism. And only God was big enough to receive the gifts offered to Him; only He was tender and understanding enough to appreciate all that stumbling, pathetic, heroic humanity held out to Him again and again. And it was God alone who knew how to gather up every least little drop of this poured-out offering into something big, and everlasting, and beautiful beyond any dreams to conceive.

"Sometimes," she went on again falteringly, "I seem to get a glimpse of what I want. I seem to feel something bigger, and more tender, and infinitely more understanding than anything I could ever have thought of. Something—*Someone*—who appreciated and loved Dickie and his gift more, far more, than even I did. Someone to whom you would want to give your whole self, even though it did mean weeks and weeks of agony. That is what I *seem* to glimpse"—she was crying now—"and that is what I want you to say is true."

"It is true! It is true!" He almost shouted the words. It was the triumphant cry of a great revelation. "And infinitely more than that is true."

He poured out a torrent of words, of assurance, of faith, of hope and joy. His face shone with conviction, and he spoke as he had not spoken even in Saint John's that day; and all the time he felt that it was not himself speaking, it was the infinite tenderness of the God who cared, striving to break through for her consolation and help.

❧

They rose at last and went down the path together.

"You have given me so much more than I ever hoped for," she said, tremulous with gratitude and happiness.

"But you have made a greater gift to me," he answered solemnly.

She looked up astonished, but she was too exhausted now to try to understand further.

"It does not seem possible that I could ever have given *you* anything," she said simply; "but if I did, it was only what my son gave to me."

"You gave to me, and your son gave to you, as mine gives to me," he returned. "We are all making extraordinary gifts to one another in these great and terrible days. It is the flaming gift of humanity, that God inspires mankind to give to mankind."

She did not understand, but he had given her what she needed, and much more, and she went away content and deeply fortified. Presently, back in the little summerhouse, Thomas McCord saw her car dart away down the white road and speed off, and off again, into the distance. But now, for him, the whole world was changed. It was filled once more, replete and overflowing with the great Presence, and there was, as well, the infinitely dear and close companionship of his boy.

For a time he sat still, swept away on great tides of love and joy and healing. Then at length he drew forth the letter once more. In this moment of exaltation he could bear to face the full details of his son's death. His eye ran hastily down the lines, until they came at last to the cry, "I'm blind! I can't see a thing!"

"I would not tell you this," the letter continued, "if it were not for what came afterward. Your son was very brave, and presently he got himself together and began to talk about you, and how you had been everything to him, father and mother both. He wanted to dictate a letter to you, but before I could get back with the writing materials, he had gone to you himself. They said his mind wandered, but I knew it wasn't wandering; it was just where it wanted to be. He was going with you all about the old places, the village, the church, and the garden—most of all the garden. Have you a mockingbird that sits up on the chimney and sings? He heard him all the time and kept laughing and calling to you to listen. And is there an especial clump of daffodils that he called his?" (There was! there was! They were blooming now, not ten feet from the summerhouse.) "He said, 'Look, Dad, my daffodils always bloom first.' But he kept wondering why it was so dark. And then all at once he saw something, I don't know what, but he flung out his arms wide and cried, 'The *light!* The *light,* Father! Look at the light!' I never in my life heard such joy and triumph in any voice—it rang through the whole ward. And that is really all. He was quiet soon after that, and just slept away."

Thomas McCord laid down the letter, and the great relieving tears—the first he had shed—rushed down his cheeks and shook him all over.

The light! The light! Yes, he would look at it where it had been freshly revealed to him in this flaming hour, there in the heart of great, suffering, heroic humanity. The heroism of all the world—glorious young humanity standing firm on the battlefields, and little gray unnoticed humanity being steadfast at home. Only God could have awakened it, only God, to whom all hearts are open, and all desires known, could ever comprehend it all. Alone in his garden, yet not alone, he seemed to feel the outpouring of mankind going up in waves of devotion and self-surrender, to be received by an infinite understanding, an infinite compassion and love; the offering and the response—the great antiphonal of the world.

He rose up and stood in the fading light, his face raised in adoration. "There is nothing, nothing of any of us that is ever lost to Thee, my Lord," he whispered. "Every drop of our being, every smallest offering that we ever make, is known of Thee and gathered up into thy everlasting treasuries; and Thou—the Gift of all our hearts—art worthy beyond all power to express, of the uttermost that a man may offer. And tomorrow, my Lord, if it is acceptable unto Thee, and if Thou wilt give me the strength, I will speak to my people, not from any of the old texts, but from the new book of courage and hope, which, freshly inspired by Thee in these transcendent days, is being written page by page, by mankind, for mankind. And with Thy help, the words of my text shall be the words of my son: 'The light! The light, Father! Look at the light!'"

MARGARET PRESCOTT MONTAGUE *(1878–1955), born in White Sulphur Springs, West Virginia, was one of the more prolific authors of the first third of the twentieth century, writing books such as* The Poet, Miss Kate and I *(1905),* The Sowing of Alderson Cree *(1907),* Closed Doors *(1915),* The Gift *(1919),* England to America *(1920),* Deep Channel *(1923), and* The Lucky Lady *(1933), as well as many short stories.*

TEN

Pieces of Silver

Clarence Budington Kelland

Carnavon, an orator of rare ability, had the power to make skeptics of even the most devout believers, so persuasive was his eloquence and reasoning.

Then came a knock on his hotel door. An old man stood there. An old man who likened him to that long-ago Saul of Tarsus.

❧

Ordinary men and women—shopkeepers, artisans, doctors, lawyers, clerks—made Carnavon's audience, and he held them breathless, spellbound. They leaned forward in their seats, all two thousand of them intent on each vibrant word. In obedience to his genius they swayed with laughter, rewarded his pathos with tears, gasped at the daring of his conclusions. And yet, he attacked what many of them held most dear—their God.

From the instant of Carnavon's appearance on the platform the audience had been his, conquered before he uttered a word by the potency of his presence, by the excellence of his physical self, by the magnificence of the animal. At his first utterance there seemed to arise a collective sigh, and thenceforward until he ceased speaking his hearers were not their own, but Carnavon's.

The showman moves his puppets with invisible threads, so that they dance and posture and contort themselves as he wills; Carnavon's invisible threads reached not from his fingers to the limbs of his audience, but from his mind to their brains and hearts—and they comported themselves according to his desires. He was such an orator as the world hears only once in many generations. He held sacred matters dangling before men and women in whom religion had been planted and watered from the cradle; yet under his relentless logic, his flashing wit, his acid irony, they shriveled and crackled to ashes and were sacred no more. Out of curiosity, men firm in their faith came to see and hear him; they departed doubting God, if not denying Him, groping for a foothold in a world the orator had deprived of its firm foundation. This thing Carnavon did for a price—one thousand dollars a lecture.

After his address, Carnavon returned to the hotel and went at once to his apartment. Scarcely had he made himself comfortable with a book, when a knock sounded at his door.

"Come in," he said.

The door opened reluctantly, and Carnavon was startled to see on his threshold an old man—embarrassed and hesitating, white of hair, with patriarchal beard, clothed in the garb of the Salvation Army.

"Mr. Carnavon," he said diffidently, "may I come in?"

Carnavon recovered himself and motioned to a chair. "How can I serve you?" he asked, rising with always ready courtesy.

The old man paused a moment and fumbled with the visor of his cap before replying. "You can give a few of the many minutes yet before you to an old man whose course is nearly run," he said at length, and his voice was singularly gentle, "a few minutes leavened with patience."

Carnavon bowed assent and again motioned to a chair, which the old man declined, although he smiled in the declining.

"I heard you speak tonight," he said. "You were like the picture I have loved to envision of young Saul of Tarsus before his feet trod the road to Damascus."

Carnavon was astonished. Not infrequently had he

been compelled to listen privately to his opponents, to ministers of the gospel, to zealots who forced themselves upon him to convert or condemn. To all alike, whether they came in humility and love or in heat and with invective on their lips, he had comported himself with the same dignity, the same courtesy, the same self-restraint. But none had been like this little old man in uniform; about none had hovered this spirit of gentle sweetness, of fatherly affection.

"Sir," continued the aged warrior of God's Army of the Streets, "I have not come hoping to convert you to my belief. You are a greater man than I, blessed with greater gifts, and I could not prevail. I have come to ask you a question: Sir, are you sincere? Do you believe in your heart the things you say with your lips?"

"If I did not," replied Carnavon, "I should remain silent."

"Sir," he said presently, "can perfect sincerity and one thousand dollars a lecture go hand in hand? When I am gone, I ask you to consider this. One, believing in the Master, betrayed Him for thirty pieces of silver; you, not believing in Him, cannot betray Him, but you war on Him with the weapons He gave you—for many times thirty pieces of silver. With your honest unbelief, I have no quarrel; when you pass it on to others for gain, you do an evil thing. God may forgive the honest doubt—the thirty pieces of silver He cannot forget."

The stranger spoke as to one he loved, without rancor, softening criticism with gentleness. Carnavon was not offended; indeed, he was moved, but he waited, making no reply. Again the old man spoke, this time as he retired toward the door.

"Sir, I have liked to think of Saul as I see you. So have I pictured him when he went out in his young strength against the followers of the Master. He traveled his road to Damascus and saw his vision. One day a vision may come to you." He paused in the open door and stretched out his hand with the gesture of one who asks a thrice-valued favor. "If the vision comes and I am yet alive, will you seek me out? I have not far to go before my race is done, but that would be sweet knowledge for me to carry with me."

Carnavon rose, smiling the smile that drew men to him. "If Saul sees his vision and becomes Paul, he will come to you," he said.

Then the door closed on the ancient soldier of peace, and he was gone.

Carnavon, having no heaven to look forward to, strove to make his plot of earth more beautiful. His home, a structure to delight the fancy, stood among acres whose loveliness was wrought by art that aided and followed, rather than sought to lead, nature. Within the house, wherever the eye rested, were paintings, statues, tapestries, furnishings that made one eager for a longer scrutiny. Vases of exquisite form, antiques from the hands of long-dead masters, medallions wrought by the great Cellini himself, made splendid nook and niche. Indeed, Carnavon loved his medals with particular affection; they were his avocation, they and their baser kindred born to commerce: coins.

No common coin-collector was he; not for age or rarity or country did he seek, but for beauty alone. A coin no bigger than the nail of one's finger, if it but presented the face of beauty, gave him greater joy than a canvas made immortal by Titian or a statue hewn by the chisel of Michelangelo.

As he sat in the library one evening, a servant entered, saying, "There is a man at the door who asks to see you. It is about a coin, sir—a rare coin, he says."

"Show him in," said Carnavon.

He arose as the caller entered. The man was of doubtful age, evidently a Hebrew. "Mr. Carnavon, I have brought for your inspection a rare and beautiful, by my estimation, coin. I understand you are interested in such."

"Yes, provided they *are* beautiful."

The Hebrew drew a tiny parcel from his pocket, removed a paper wrapping, and disclosed a small metal box. Raising its cover, he extracted a small silver coin and extended it to Carnavon.

The master of the house accepted it and moved closer to the light, scrutinizing it intently. A puzzled expression crossed his face. "I have never seen a similar piece," he said. "Indeed, I must confess I cannot identify it. Will you do so for me?"

"It is Hebrew coinage," explained the dealer. "You will observe in relief the olive branch and the pot of manna. Simon the High Priest had authority to stamp and issue it. Nineteen hundred odd years, you see, is its age, yet it is wonderfully preserved and scarcely worn. I have handled thousands of coins, but none of such antiquity not worn almost to obliteration.

"It is rarely beautiful," admitted Carnavon. "I should like to possess it. What price do you set?"

"Though I am a dealer, I am at a loss to give it value. Allow me to leave it with you for a few days, not as a coin, but as an article of value. At the end of that time, make me an offer."

It was a strange enough proposition, yet fair, and Carnavon instantly acceded. The Hebrew expressed thanks and took his departure. Carnavon moved to the inviting depths of a huge chair before the glowing log in the fireplace and, holding the coin of Simon the High Priest in his palm, leaned forward to possess its beauties all the better. Over and over he turned it, marking its perfection of design, the miracle of its preservation. A coin of Simon the High Priest! What scenes were limned at the mention of his name! It was Carnavon's profession to jeer at inconsistencies in the epic of the Passion, to tear it part from part with the scalpel of his remorseless logic; but to deny its poetic beauty must be left to someone other than he. It was his custom to refer to it as the greatest fiction in the world.

An hour he spent thus, delighting in his new possession. At last, raising his eyes at the sudden darkening of the room, he saw that the room was no longer about him. He was standing in a great court, stone paved, high walled, porticoed, and majestically before him rose the pile of a great building, its successive terraces lifting upward and upward in awful grandeur. Carnavon gazed, incredulous, for the outline of the structure was familiar to him. He knew he was standing in the shadow of Solomon's Porch, in the Court of the Gentiles of Herod's Temple in Jerusalem.

As he marveled, a man, furtive of action, appeared from the direction of the Gate of Coponius and strode rapidly inside the confines marked by the walls, beyond which no Gentile dare pass on pain of death. Yet Carnavon was drawn to follow.

Within, pacing up and down in the shadow, was an imposing presence priestly robed, wearing the insignia of the High Priest, and toward him the furtive stranger hastened. Carnavon stood in the shelter of a pillar and listened.

"I have come," the stranger murmured.

"It is well," replied the High Priest, drawing away his garment. "Wilt thou do the thing?"

"I will do it," whispered the man, and shuddered in the speaking.

"By what sign shall my soldiers know Him whom we seek? Perchance they may mistake another for Him. But thou goest with them to show the way and the place. When thou hast come unto Him, go thou to His side and kiss Him on the cheek as a sign that He is the man and none other." There was scorn in the voice of Simon the High Priest. He turned on his heel and would have departed, but the furtive one clutched his mantle and detained him. Simon frowned back into that face distorted by avarice, and his eyes grew hard.

"Truly," said the High Priest, "I had forgotten thy wage." And forthwith he drew a bag from the folds of his upper garment. He counted money into the hand of the man, and Carnavon counted with him. Thirty times did the fingers of the High Priest enter the bag, and thirty times did the pieces of silver drop into the outstretched, trembling claw. The last of the thirty fell from the overflowing palm and rolled to Carnavon's feet, resting in a spot of moonlight. It glittered whitely—and in distinct relief the familiar pot of manna was visible; in every respect it was the fellow of the coin Carnavon still grasped in his hand.

Carnavon looked again, and the temple was not there, neither was the furtive one, nor the High Priest. All about him stretched light-dotted darkness; in the distance toward the city, the mingled voices of approaching tumult affronted the night. Presently, a throng armed with swords and staves hurried and jostled along the road, led by the furtive stranger of the temple, his black beard sunk on his breast. Carnavon was compelled to follow them.

Soon they left the beaten road, and on a hillside they came upon a little group of men in the midst of whom stood a figure erect, bare of head and calm. To the side of this central figure the furtive one pushed his way and cried out in an awful voice, hoarse, fearful, quivering, "Master,

Master!" and kissed Him on the cheek. As he moved, Carnavon could hear the sound of silver pieces jingling together in his garment.

The Master spoke softly, calmly, with infinite sorrow. "Judas,"—His eyes rested an instant on the cringing figure—"betrayest thou the Son of Man with a kiss?"

Cries of dismay rose weakly from the little group, and they fell away—all save one, who drew his sword and threw himself on those threatening the Master, severing the ear from the head of one of them. The Master touched the place with His finger, and it was healed.

Carnavon looked again, and it was daylight in the court of Herod's Temple. He passed inward and stood with an assembly about the High Priest—men of weight and dignity, the priests and elders of the people. As he watched them, heads together, discussing some matter of import, there came again the furtive one, now changed by remorse, by terror, so that his face was painful to look upon. He approached the High Priest, saying, "I have sinned—I have betrayed innocent blood!" He fell to his knees, his hands full of silver.

The High Priest looked on him coldly and replied in even tones, "What is that to us? See thou to that."

Whereupon the furtive one flung the silver from him wildly and rushed out of the temple. Carnavon followed until they came to a lonely place, and there the man hanged himself from a tree so that his feet dangled over a precipice.

Again Carnavon stood upon a bare, forbidding hillside among a shouting, gesticulating throng. From the apex of the hill arose three crosses. Carnavon covered his face, for the sight was cruel.

From the mob of shouting people jeers and gibes arose. One man, more conspicuous than his fellows, strode near the foot of the central cross and cried, "For thirty pieces of silver was He sold—this King of the Jews. Doth not a slave bring more?" And he continued to utter gibes and ridicule. At last the Man opened His eyes and regarded his tormentor, not with anger, not rebukingly, but with majestic calm. It was not a glance to strike terror; it conveyed no anger, no threat; but the tormentor fell silent, awed by its divine loftiness.

It seemed to Carnavon that the Master's eyes sought him out and touched him for an instant, and he sank to the ground, crouching in awe, and hiding his face from the eyes of Him he had persecuted.

Carnavon raised himself to his feet from the depths of his chair before the blazing fire and passed his hand across his eyes as though to wipe away a film. Then, without movement, he stood staring into the blaze, his face a mask. And so he remained until the log was embers and the blaze a glow. He sighed. His features changed from stoniness to grief, and he raised the hand in which was clasped the piece of silver and the coinage of Simon, opened it and, bowing his head, gazed reverently on a sacred thing.

Swiftly his bearing altered to determination, to action. He thrust on his coat, his hat, and went out into the night, traversing road and street until he came to the crowded places of the city where men turned night into day. And as he walked he listened. Faintly, borne to his ear on the chill wind, came the sound of singing, of instruments of music, of drums, and he smiled.

In a public square huddled a shivering squalid crowd, its nucleus a little band of uniformed soldiers of the Cross—men and women. As Carnavon approached, the music ceased. A small, tottering old man, silvery of hair and beard, doffed his cap and stepped to the center of the circle, raising his hand for silence. Carnavon had found whom he sought; it was the stranger of the hotel room.

Carnavon made his way through the fringe of idle listeners, swayed to the side of the praying old man, and, urged to impatience by emotion, waited not for him to cease. He clutched an extended hand and cried in a broken voice, "I have sinned—I have betrayed innocent blood!"

The old preacher of the streets paused, looked on Carnavon's face, and over his wrinkled features spread a look of perfect peace, of richest happiness.

"You...you have stood on the road to Damascus?" he whispered, his hands groping for Carnavon's.

"Yes, and I have seen a vision."

The old man smiled. "Saul has become Paul."

CLARENCE BUDINGTON KELLAND *(1881-1964), born in Portland, Michigan, was editor of* American Boy *for a time and one of the most prolific and best-selling writers of his day. Among his books are* Sudden Jim, Arizona, *and* Merchant of Valor.

ELEVEN

Lilies for Inspiration

Mabel McKee

Oh how Emily yearned for that jade hat for Easter. Maybe then the handsome soloist, Warren Blaine, would notice her.

But oh, the difference that Easter lily might make in an old man's life! Which would it be: self, or sacrifice for others? What tipped the balance was a paragraph in her mother's most recent letter.

Fate placed the florist shop next door to the hat shop. Emily Rowe was sure of that. She was just ready to go into the shop to buy the jade green hat when she saw the perfect Easter lily.

If only it had not been so perfect, she would not have gone into the florist shop to see it better. In that case the exquisite green hat, which seemed to have been made for her auburn hair, would not have been sold to the college girl rather than to her.

The owner of the hat store tried to interest Emily in other hats that were just as pretty as the jade green one had been. Emily was not interested in any of them. Madame of the store was plainly irritated at her attitude. She did not know that on the single occasion when Warren Blaine had noticed Emily as anyone more than the secretary to the radio station manager, he had spoken of her "glorious hair." Madame had not heard him say: "You would be stunning in a jade hat."

Madame might have heard Warren Blaine's voice, however. Myriads of people who listened in on the evenings he broadcast knew him as their favorite. He received many times as many letters as did other artists at the studio. As secretary to the manager Emily was in a position to know that.

"They *should* outnumber the others," Emily wrote her mother about Warren Blaine. "His voice is perfect. Praise and attention haven't spoiled him the least bit."

If Mother had been close to Emily she would have learned other things. She might even have heard her

daughter tell her own mirrored self, "He just simply doesn't see you with gorgeous Marcia Barlow so near."

Back at the studio a little later Emily glimpsed Warren Blaine as he passed through the office on his way into the studio. He did not even see her. Marcia, whose dusky hair and eyes seemed even more of a midnight hue under the lovely new scarlet felt hat, had all his attention.

Emily watched them through her office, then stared at the door that swung shut after them until a thin hand timidly touched her own and a frightened voice asked, "Do you mind if I carry your vase of roses into the studio with me for our hour? Flowers always soothe and inspire me when I'm nervous."

A desire to jerk her hand away from the almost claw-like fingers seized Emily. It was followed by another to say, *Why be nervous? You're just the violinist in the orchestra, you know.* She stifled both. The stooped, white-haired violinist was pitiful now, but once he had been a well-known virtuoso, wealthy and famous. She could not be other than kind to him.

"They're really Mr. Walton's roses," she said. "But I'm sure he'd be glad to loan them to you."

Right then the office boy tossed a fresh pile of letters onto her desk. Mother's creamy envelope fell from the pile, and Emily seized it. Her quick fingers tore it open, and for several minutes all the happenings of the studio were lost to her. She was again in the pretty little yellow parsonage in Lindendale, sniffing the jonquils and the narcissuses that her mother grew so there would be Easter flowers for the entire house.

She was seeing other things in that home, as Mother's letter described them: the birthday cake for twelve-year-old Alice, Janet's first party dress, Jerry's topcoat, and Father's new suit. "The bishop will be here for Easter to hear Father preach. I have had my gray silk crepe made over and added touches of rose. You'd like the rose against my white hair."

Mother was wearing her old dress so Father could have the new suit. Mother with her beautiful white hair!

A trembling hand reached in front of Emily again. The violinist was reaching for the bowl of roses. With a little spring Emily was on her feet, smiling at the old man who had hair like her mother's. "I'll carry them for you," she offered.

The old man smiled as he walked beside Emily to the studio door. Just as they reached it, the door opened to allow Warren Blaine and Marcia Barlow, his accompanist, to pass through, their broadcast hour being over.

Emily carried the bowl of roses into the room and placed them on the piano so that they were quite near the seat the violinist would occupy. When she came back to the office, Warren Blaine had gone. Mother's letter was unfinished, however, so she was soon back in parsonage land.

"That reminds me," Mother wrote, "I want you to write the twins a letter, Emily dear, telling them that you're proud of them. They had saved up money for their class rings but bought the cheaper pins instead so they could buy a lily for the chancel for Easter Sunday. Father happened to remark that he hoped someone would bring one to the church for the occasion since it would inspire him to better delivery of his sermon."

Emily frankly let the tears shine in her lovely gray-green eyes. After a little she read on in Mother's letter, "I'm listening in every evening to your tenor soloist, dear. His voice is perfect. It makes him seem nearer to know that you and he are friends."

Friends! Of course Mother would think they were friends. Emily's letters contained so many references to Warren Blaine. The girl wondered what Mother would say about Marcia's attitude of ownership toward him and the quick, businesslike way he talked to Emily, the manager's secretary.

Emily patted Mother's letter. "Darling Jerry and Jean!" she murmured aloud.

"Lucky Jerry and Jean to have someone so beautiful to call them darling," said a teasing, wavering voice. The violinist had brought the bowl of roses back to her desk. His playing had been flawless. The director had praised him, and once again he was happy and confident. "I'm wagering that Jerry is a handsome young man who appreciates a beautiful girl with auburn curls," he added.

Emily dimpled. "He is all that," she laughed. "Jerry and Jean are just seventeen. They're my twin brother and sister." Proudly then she told him about the Easter lily they had bought for Father and the sacrifice it entailed.

"They are replicas of their big sister," said the violinist slowly. After a moment's silence he sighed softly to himself. "Easter lilies! There were masses of them at the cathedral in France when I played on Easter Sunday. All gifts to me, Fritz Tulane, who now has to borrow a bowl of roses for inspiration!"

His white head dropped again. He shuffled across the room to his worn topcoat, donned it, and, carrying his precious violin, left the room.

Behind him a sense of gloom pervaded. Although she worked feverishly revising the Easter program, that gloom hung over Emily until Enos Walton, manager of the studio, came back from the Rotary banquet.

"You've done wonders." His quick eye went over the finished program, the letters in neat piles. "By the way, Mrs. Walton told me to ask you up to the house Sunday for an Easter dinner. She's having a few friends from the studio—Warren Blaine, Professor Langford, little Billy Nance, and Fritz Tulane."

"Marcia?" Emily began.

The manager shook his head. "The missus thinks the accompanist high hats her. Women are funny that way," he finished.

All the way home Emily was thrilled. Warren Blaine and she would be together on Easter. "I must find a jade hat tomorrow," she planned.

Jade green hats of just the right shape and size for a head covered with masses of thick auburn hair are difficult to find. Emily knew that before the next morning was over. After visiting five shops, at each of which her quest had been unsuccessful, she decided to go back to the one next door to the florist shop. Perhaps she could have made a replica of the one she had seen in the window the day before.

Slowly she walked along the street. That was how she happened to again see the perfect Easter lily in the florist shop window. That was how she happened to think of the aged violinist and the inspiration flowers always brought to him.

He was to play in all the Easter morning numbers at the studio. There was one selection that contained a violin solo. "He needs Easter lilies to carry him back to the cathedral days," Emily breathed.

There in the window was the perfect Easter lily, which cost just the amount she had saved from her small salary for her jade hat. Tragically she sighed, "Just one Easter lily couldn't inspire him."

Something seemed to insist, "But this one is so beautiful, like the one the twins are buying for Father."

Nervously Emily turned from the florist's window to walk up and down the street. The conflict in her heart was raging, the struggle between a girl's desire for a jade hat and her longing to help inspire the old violinist so that he would have success again, and after that security and comfort for the coming years.

Jean and Jerry's gift to Father, the sacrifice it had entailed, Mother's joy over it, these thoughts brought her decision finally. There was a smile on her face when Emily entered the florist shop. "I want to buy the Easter lily in the window," she said. "And I want it sent to station WLOB early Sunday morning, before seven o'clock. I'll write the greeting after the lily arrives."

"You are a singer." The old man was rubbing his hands together happily. "Or perhaps you play the violin. It is so beautiful in the orchestra numbers. I listen in every evening."

"I'm just secretary to the manager," Emily smiled back at him. "But the lily is for the violinist. He is very old, and flowers inspire him. Once," Emily's voice was tender, "once he played for kings."

Carefully the florist wrote Emily's name. He assured the girl that the lily would be sent just as she directed. He then asked her to wait a minute while he went to the ice-box in which he kept special flowers. When he returned, he carried a beautiful shoulder corsage in which Talisman rosebuds and hyacinths vied in sending out their fragrance.

He pinned it to Emily's coat. "I made it just a little while ago," he said. "I was hoping that someone very beautiful would come in to wear it away. No one with a more beautiful face or soul will ever come to this store, I am sure; no one who will know so well that Easter is a day for the lifting up of dead hopes, ambitions, love, and faith and doing it as Christ Himself did when He was on earth."

Emily's voice broke, "Thank you, oh, thank you with all my heart!"

Hurried days, hurried hours, hurried minutes followed at the studio. Sometimes they were strained ones when some of the artists claimed discrimination had been shown on the studio programs when numbers had to be changed because of the demands of advertisers who financed the studio.

Finally it was Easter morning. Emily stopped at the little church on the corner for a few minutes on her way to the studio. The soft music, the lilies on the chancel, brought a wonderful peace to her heart.

Soon she was at the studio placing the beautiful Easter lily near the place where the old violinist would sit to play. The card on it bore his name and the inscription, "From one of your audience."

Emily was at her desk when Mr. Walton entered. "Child, I forgot to tell you today was a holiday for you. Don't you want to go to church?"

"Oh," Emily clasped her hands together, "I'll hurry back home in time to hear our Easter program."

Back at her rooming house, Emily turned the dial of the radio in the deserted living room until she had her own station. The music of the first Easter hymn was just starting. Leaning back in a low rocking chair she closed her eyes to listen. Soon she heard the perfect notes of Fritz Tulane's violin. When his solo came, it was so perfect that it sounded like music from heaven.

Emily could imagine the imperative ringing of the studio telephone, the telegrams, the letters, all for Fritz Tulane. A voice called her back to the room. Warren Blaine was singing "He Is Risen," singing it not only with his rich tenor voice but from a heart that put faith and hope and love in every word he uttered.

When she started through the hall, Emily saw the great box from the florist shop. On the top was the name of the shop at which the lily had been bought.

Inside were sweetheart roses and forget-me-nots, myriads of them. Right in the center of them was Warren Blaine's card. Written on it was, "I'll call for you at eleven o'clock. It's such a beautiful morning that I thought maybe you'd ride with me to take some flowers to a few old ladies who were my mother's friends."

As they drove down Sheridan Avenue, Warren told Emily about his visit to the florist shop for hyacinths for his sister. "The florist told me about your buying the Easter lily for Fritz Tulane. That was like my Mother. She died last May. It seemed to me I couldn't sing an Easter hymn today.

"I was just ready to ask the manager to substitute some other singer for me this morning when I happened to go to the florist shop and heard about your purchase of the lily to inspire Fritz. I knew then that Easter meant to you what it did to Mother—a day to help raise dead faith and hopes."

His voice grew more tender. "I knew then that you, so beautiful, so wonderfully unselfish, could inspire faith in me so that I could sing the Easter song."

They were driving through the park when they saw the old violinist walking along like a person on wings. One of the Easter lily blossoms was pinned to his coat. He was again the successful virtuoso.

"He'll never get to the Walton home in time for dinner," said Emily. "Let's take him with us."

Warren Blaine guided his car to the old man. "Yes, and I think I'd like to have him know first of all that you and I shall spend all Easters together."

MABEL MCKEE, *early in the twentieth century, was responsible for some of the most memorable inspirational literature in print. Sadly, little is known of her today.*

TWELVE

A Glimpse of Heaven

Harriet Lummis Smith

The papers screamed the news: *Claude Rockwell Commits Suicide.* Rockwell: young, good-looking, and extremely wealthy, felt that life was a cruel joke.

On the other hand, here is Mark, blind from birth, and *happy!*

What did it all mean? Now, on the eve of Easter, Mark experiences a miracle. But then…was Easter, too, a "cruel joke"?

The early edition of the morning paper was being sold at the street corners when Roland started home at midnight. Headlines running across the entire front page announced Claude Rockwell's suicide. Ronald read the announcement

with a queer feeling as though the bottom had dropped out of something; once on the streetcar, he devoured the columns devoted to the tragedy.

Roland had not known Claude Rockwell personally, but he had heard about him ever since he could remember. The Rockwells were one of the wealthiest families of the city, socially prominent. In June, Claude was to have been graduated from one of the leading eastern universities, and it had been generally understood that he would spend a year in travel before taking up his work. He had gone on a longer journey, however.

He had left a letter in his room explaining what he was about to do. "Having made up my mind," he wrote, "that life is a cruel joke inflicted on the helpless, I see no reason to endure it longer." He had then signed his full name and written the date. He was just twenty-two.

Roland slept poorly that night. The tragedy of Claude Rockwell's life and death seemed to have become his own. Claude apparently had everything that life could give him, but it had not been enough. He was bored, disillusioned, embittered. Roland turned on his pillow and tried in vain to sleep.

When he went down to breakfast, heavy eyed and disinclined for food, his father and mother were discussing the tragedy. "Crazy, of course," Mr. Craig was saying. "There never was a more unreasonable suicide. Why, that boy had everything anyone could ask for."

Mrs. Craig sighed. "His father and mother must be heartbroken."

Roland stole a sidelong glance at her. Despite the shadow on her face caused by the distressing news, Mrs. Craig had the appearance of a happy woman. Roland looked at his father. Mr. Craig was just fifty and the hair at his temples was noticeably gray; but his clear eyes showed no distrust of the future.

They've found life good, thought Roland. *And yet they've worked hard and done without a lot of things other folks have. I suppose their being Christians makes the difference. And yet, who is right? Is life a blessing or is it a joke?*

The arrival of the morning mail turned their thoughts abruptly into another channel. It brought a letter from Mrs. Craig's sister, and its news was startling.

"We're bringing Mark to the city next week," Mrs. Pryor wrote. "We have been urged to take him to Dr. Williams, a young man who is credited with doing some very wonderful things. It seems too much to hope that he can do anything for Mark, but of course we do not want to leave a stone unturned."

Mrs. Craig, reading the letter aloud, stopped abruptly and looked across the table at her husband. "Poor Lillian!" she said.

Mr. Craig nodded. "Yes, I'm sorry they're trying it," he answered. "A hope, even a faint one, makes the inevitable all the harder to bear."

"But, of course, if there was a chance in a million, they'd want to take it," Mrs. Craig exclaimed.

"But there can't be a chance, my dear. Mark was born blind, and now—why, he's as old as you are, Roland, isn't he?"

"A little older, Father. He was twenty-one last October."

As a result of that letter, Roland started thinking of his cousin Mark rather than of Claude Rockwell. Suddenly he found himself comparing the two. Mark apparently had been as unfortunate as Claude had been fortunate. Born blind, he had been denied the normal pleasures of boyhood, yet somehow he had achieved a sunniness of disposition that caused his associates to marvel.

The next few days were hectic for the Craig family. Dr. Williams did not say he could do anything for Mark. Indeed, although he promised nothing, he intimated that there were strong grounds for being hopeful. Mark remained at the hospital after the examination, and when Roland saw him that first evening, he seemed curiously calm.

Three days after his arrival in the city, the operation took place. Another three days went by and then, shortly after Roland reached the office, he was called to the telephone. His mother was speaking. "Oh, Roland!" Her voice shook hysterically. "The operation has been successful."

"What!" exclaimed Roland. "You don't mean—"

"Yes, Mark can see. Of course they are very cautious at first, so as not to overtax his eyes; but he can see."

At the Craig home, a little later, Mark had his first glimpse of the outdoor world. It was a Sunday afternoon, and all the family were present.

After dinner they adjourned to the living room. Mark, taking off the shade he had worn over his eyes during the meal, walked to the window and stood looking out. They waited tensely for what he would say.

"So that's what the sky's like. So that's what they mean by blue." He faced about, and the tears were running down his cheeks. For all his infirmity, Mark was a stalwart young fellow, broad-shouldered, deep-chested. His tears startled them all.

Roland crossed the room with two strides, and flung his arms around his cousin's shoulders. "Steady, old chap. It's nothing to cry about. You'll get used to it in no time."

Mark wiped his eyes, blew his nose, and achieved a husky laugh. "Well, I hope not. My, but that was wonderful. I've talked about the sky all my life and didn't know what I meant." His gaze fell on a vase on the mantel. "Those are roses, aren't they?"

"Yes."

"I recognized the odor, but I didn't know they looked like that. Why, color is the most marvelous thing on earth. It must be great to be an artist."

As the surgeon wished to see his patient frequently for a time, it was decided that Mark and his mother should remain at the Craigs' until after Easter. They all enjoyed watching Mark get acquainted with the world in which he had lived for twenty-one years. His enthusiasm over common objects thrilled them, although it amused them too. His excitement over the first dandelion he had ever seen, his rapture over a peach tree in bloom, his wonder and delight when a bluebird flew past the window were things Roland could never forget.

Roland was late getting away from the office the Saturday before Easter. He stopped at the florist's for flowers for his mother, and then boarded a streetcar for home.

His mother was in the living room as Roland entered. He went toward her smiling and then stopped with a jerk. His flowers fell to the floor beside him, and he did not notice them. His mother's eyes were swollen with long weeping. "Mother! What is it?" Even as he asked the question, he knew.

"Mark is blind again. He was taking a short walk with his mother, and enjoying everything the way he does, you know, and all at once he stopped and said, 'Mother, it's all dark.' She brought him home and telephoned the doctor. He said to bring him right to the hospital. I went with them, of course, but I'm afraid from the way he talked, that he has very little hope. Mark took it very quietly, but poor Lillian—" For the first time Mrs. Craig noticed the florist's box on the floor. "What is that, dear? Were you bringing me flowers?"

"Yes, I was, but let them lie there and wither." The sound of his own voice startled him. "Flowers, in a world where such things can happen."

"Oh, Roland!"

"I mean it, Mother. All that's beautiful is a mockery. Poor Claude Rockwell was in the right. Life's a joke, a cruel one.

In the morning Mrs. Pryor was unable to leave her bed. "You'll go to the hospital this morning and stay with Mark, won't you?" Mrs. Craig asked her son.

"Oh, I suppose so. I dread seeing him till he's had time to get over this disappointment. But I guess if he can stand it, I can."

Roland was later in getting away from the house than he meant to be, and already the streets were full of people on their way to church. Spring costumes replaced the heavy garb of winter. As he passed one of the downtown churches, the throbbing notes of a great organ set the air vibrating about him.

Eternal life! That was what the jubilant notes of the organ meant. That was back of all this stir, these new garments, whether people were conscious of it or not. *I should think they'd get enough of it right here in this world*, thought Roland savagely, *without going on and on through eternity.*

He reached the hospital at last. Mark's room was darkened, and his eyes were bandaged. The young man turned on his pillow as his cousin entered, recognizing his step. "That you, Roland?"

Roland crossed the room and gripped Mark's hand. He could not trust himself to speak.

"I thought you'd go to church this morning, but I was expecting Mother."

"Aunt Lillian's not feeling quite herself this morning," Roland said. "But I guess she'll be over this afternoon."

"Find a chair and make yourself comfortable, Roland. Yes, poor Mother, I know she's terribly disappointed."

Roland found it impossible to reply. After waiting a moment, as though for him to speak, Mark went on rather wistfully. "As far as I'm concerned, I never expected the operation would be successful. I came because Mother wished it, but I was the most astonished chap on earth when I found I could really see. And even though it has turned out this way, I can't get over thinking how lucky I am."

"*Lucky!*" Roland was sorry as soon as the exclamation escaped him.

"Look at it this way, Roland. I was born blind. I've lived blind for twenty-one years. A month ago I'd have laughed at anyone who suggested I might see, and now I'm back where I was then, except for one thing. I've had a few days of vision. I know what the sky is like when it's blue, and at night when it's spangled with stars. I've seen the green of the grass and the beauty of the flowers. I didn't have my eyesight long enough to grow dependent on it, but it has made me richer by a lot of wonderful memories. I know better than I did what the world I live in is like. And it almost seems," Mark ended with a little laugh, "that I know what heaven is like too."

"Mark, Mark, do you mean it when you lie there and tell me you're lucky? Do you mean it, or are you just putting on? If I were in your place—perhaps I oughtn't to say it, but it's true—I'd feel that life was a cruel joke."

"Not if you took eternal life into account."

Mark spoke quietly, but something in his voice silenced Roland's outburst more effectively than if he had shouted. He turned his head, and Roland saw he was smiling. "That's the answer to all the riddles, old boy, don't you see—just that life goes on. There'll be time to finish what isn't done here, and to adjust things, and to carry everything through to a perfect consummation. You say if you were in my place, you'd think of life as a cruel joke. Well, it's not only people like me—"

"I know! I know! I was only quoting. The fellow I got it from seemed to be one of the lucky ones, but he killed himself."

"You have to take eternal life into account," Mark said again. "But if you think of your life here as an infinitesimal part of a great whole, things like my blindness and the other things that are worse won't trouble you."

There was silence in the room for a moment, but to Roland it seemed as though the pealing chords of the great organ were distinctly audible. Life meant bitterness and disillusion only to those who rejected all that Christ came to bring. To those who accepted the fullness of life He offered, the present was vital with joy, the future radiant with hope. Roland felt that for the first time in his life he understood the meaning of Easter; he, too, had caught a glimpse of heaven.

HARRIET LUMMIS SMITH *(?–1947), born in Auburndale, Massachusetts, was a prolific writer of inspirational and value-based stories early in this century. Besides writing books such as* Other People's Business *(1916), she wrote the three books in the* Peggy Raymond *series and the four later books in the* Pollyanna *series (1924–1929), as well as a large number of short stories.*

THIRTEEN

The Hollow Man

Joseph Leininger Wheeler

Oh he was handsome, beautiful as a Greek god,
But he was empty: a hollow boom-booming drum;
Oh he could speak, could sway multitudes,
But inside, where his heart should have been,
There was only sawdust, straw,
And swirling, mocking winds.

Never thought it would happen, Sylvester, Charles murmured as he buried his fingers deep in the black-and-white cat's thick, silky coat. *Life is beginning to bore me.*

What are you hungry for today, Sylvester? Are you bored with life too? Come to think of it, you do lead a boring life, imprisoned within these four walls: no wonder you sleep most of the time!

But for me, sleep doesn't bring any answers. I don't sleep well any more, unless I take sleeping pills. When I do wake up, I find myself restless, empty, reluctant to face another meaningless day.

Okay, Sylvester. Now what? Breakfast over, the day stretches out before me promising only boredom. I've run out of options. There's got to be a cure for this boredom; there always has been before. Let's see. How about a safari? No. I'm bored with safaris. Besides, it's not really sport any more: the odds are all stacked on my side. After all, how many leopard or tiger heads on the wall does it take to prove I'm a man?

Maybe deep-sea fishing off the Great Barrier Reef? Nope. That, too, seems boring now. Fighting swordfish doesn't give me much of a kick any more. Besides, they are so iridescently beautiful, so vibrantly alive one minute, and so needlessly dead a minute later. No deep-sea fishing.

All right. Let's see. Oh yes, perhaps mountain climbing would bring back some excitement into my life. K-2? No. Already climbed it. Aconcagua? No, climbed it ten—or was it eleven?—years ago. Matterhorn? Nope. Too easy. Everest? Possibly, but I've turned chicken. Can't get over those eight deaths last year, especially that of my climbing buddy, Henry. No, mountain climbing doesn't hold the answer either.

It's too early for skiing, unless I fly down to Australia. Think I'd rather not. Or some trekking in Antarctica? No. Been there twice already—and it's so bitterly cold! Of course I could outfit The Sea Princess *and head for the Canaries or Norway. No, not the answer either. Time really drags on the high seas.*

Say! Maybe I ought to run up to New York and take in a play or a concert, or maybe an exhibition; there's always so much to do and see there. But hold on, that won't work either. One sees the same crowd everywhere—all bored stiff, but trying to act sophisticatedly interested (translated, meaning ennui). No New York.

This is terrible! Here I am, able to afford anything I set my heart on—yet everything has become ho-hum. And I'm only forty-three years old! What on God's green earth am I going to do with the rest of my life?

Perhaps the answer lies in speed.

Charles taxied out to the main channel of the Severn River and gradually opened her up. Soon the deep-throated roar of *Poseidon,* his long sleek bullet of a boat, swallowed up all other sounds. It was a stunningly beautiful day on the Chesapeake, with hundreds of white sails everywhere, and almost as many speedboats. He thundered down the bay, passing everything in sight, and then stopped for lunch at old Saint Michael's. In the early evening, he nosed *Poseidon* into Ego Alley, the harbor hub of Annapolis, and tied it up on the sea wall. But this time, even the sight of the envious men and women promenading by, sighing out their longing for a boat like his, did nothing to reduce his boredom. All he could think of as he roared home up the Severn, the petrol screaming its way through the great dual turbines, was the obscenely high price tag for this childish showing off.

Sleep refused to come that night. After several hours of wide-awake tossing and turning, he gave it up as hopeless and slipped out to the dark living room. The moon shone with a ghostly sheen on the river, turning it to molten silver.

He sat down in his favorite blue chair. Sylvester found him almost instantly, purring his delight and kneading claws into his bathrobe. *Perhaps here in this chair, this night, I might come to grips with my problem and find a solution. If there indeed* is *a solution—to my loss of interest in life.* It seemed likely, this restless night, that such answers could be found only in the past. *Perhaps I should go back to the beginning.*

SUNSHINE AND THE DARK

Home. Which home? None had lasted very long, for his navy parents had moved often. *But moving didn't mean anything,* he mused, *for wherever Mom and Dad were, that was home.* Along the way, he had been joined by a brother and a sister, Anthony and Jean. The three children had been very close during those growing-up years.

Had been. During the intervening years, his vast wealth had created an ever widening chasm between them. Even their families he now barely knew. *I've missed a lot,* Charles sighed. But he didn't stop there. The answer didn't lie with Anthony or Jean.

In high school he'd been a geek, somewhat of a misfit. Not until college had he really fit in, really belonged, really been popular. In his freshman year, he had discovered girls; some he was temporarily serious about—but only one interest lasted: Elizabeth, whom everyone knew as "Sunny." She got her nickname partly because of her gloriously golden hair, and partly because she radiated happiness everywhere she was, everywhere she went.

The competition had been stiff, for she was the campus dream girl. Initially, he wanted her just because so many of the other guys did; later on, because he could not even imagine facing the rest of his life without that serene and joyful presence at his side. They had been friends first and foremost, soul mates, long before the physical need for her had become almost an ache, long before that wondrous evening when he asked her to marry him.

For some time he'd been wondering when and where he would propose. Complicating the process was her growing coolness and distancing in her responses to his ardent attentions.

The time and place turned out to be an evening cruise on the San Francisco Bay, the Saturday of Easter weekend. He had planned it for weeks, down to the last detail and the single red rose. No more romantic evening or setting could he have imagined. He had felt that her recent coolness would dissipate in the joy his proposal would bring, all uncertainties now being swept aside.

The moment came, and his voice shaking a little, he asked her that life-changing question: "Sunny, you *know* I love you—uh, uh, will…uh…you marry me?"

Never would he forget the long silence that followed. So long it seemed an eternity. Finally, initially refusing to meet his eyes, her voice ragged with intense feeling, she spoke the words that represented the dividing line between his boyhood and his manhood:

"Oh, Charlie, thank you for asking me, for honoring me…but…but—"

"But what?" he impatiently broke in.

"Oh, Charlie, I wish I didn't have to give reasons for my answer. I've known for some time you were going to ask me—and knew I'd have to give you an answer."

He stood there gripping the railing so tightly his fingers ached. The lights of San Francisco, just moments ago radiating encouragement and blessing, now seemed dim and blurry. This was not at all the way he had pictured her rapturous response! What could possibly have gone wrong?

"Oh, Charlie," she repeated, "this is not easy to do."

"Well, *do* it and get it over with," he snapped, his pride ripped to shreds. "I suppose there's someone else…more worthy of you than I am."

"Oh no! No! No! It's not that," she responded, her voice etched in pain.

"Well, what *is* it?" he demanded. "Don't you love me anymore?"

Ever so softly, she murmured, "Yes, I *do* love you, Charlie—that's what makes it so hard."

"You're not making much sense," he growled; something ugly inside him wanted to wound her.

"Oh, Charlie, it's a lot of things I'd hoped weren't true and would go away. But they haven't. You're ambitious, you want to get rich quick—"

"What's wrong with that?" he cut in.

"Nothing wrong in itself, but there's more to it than that! Your obsession with money means more to you than I do—or ever could."

"You know that's not true!"

Miserably she countered, "You know it *is* true, Charlie," and dared him, with her clear honest eyes, to deny it. His silence confirmed her words.

"More even than that," she continued, "it means more to you than *God* does!"

Still silent, Charles stared blankly out to sea.

She continued, "This is Easter weekend, Charlie. Yet you've said not one word about it and its meaning to you! I know you grew up in a Christian home, but you never speak of our Lord or of wanting to do His will or how you want to make a difference."

Frozen there to the railing, Charles returned not a word.

"Oh, Charlie!" she cried, now impassioned. "I don't even know if a heart—a *real* heart—exists inside you. You seem all facade, all mask...I've tried to find the real you. Sometimes I wonder if there's even a real you in there! You seem—pardon the expression—*hollow.*"

Those words—the last he ever heard her speak—were swallowed in his snarling response. He unleashed words of such viciousness, such cruelty, such malevolence, that she visibly withered and blanched under the onslaught and gazed at him disbelievingly, as though he were someone she had never known before.

Not one word did they say to each other during the long ride back to the campus. He turned the radio volume way up and stared straight ahead. When they arrived in front of the dormitory, she didn't wait, as usual, for him to open her door, but quietly opened it herself, slipped out, and walked out of his life without so much as one backward glance.

He left college for good the next day—and never returned. When he got home, he gave only one answer to his parents: "Sunny jilted me." Later that night, shortly after midnight, he packed the things that meant most to him, took one half-regretful look at his boyhood bedroom, loaded his car, backed down the long driveway, and sped away, out of his parents' lives. He never returned. Nor did he write, phone, or remember them with presents. Whatever personal letters caught up with him he scanned but did not answer. The past, he determined, must be wiped out of conscious memory, never to be retrieved from his subconscious. And so it had been: *never*, until this sleepless night, had he returned to it.

CROESUS

He headed straight for the oil fields of the Southwest and signed on as the greenest of the green. Behind him, he'd left whatever existed in his life of an ethical code—and God.

So, totally devoid of scruples, unconcerned about who might get hurt or even destroyed, with almost lightning speed he ruthlessly climbed over the bodies of his associates to success.

His defining moment came at last one October in the dead of night. He'd bought drilling rights to a vast tract of land on the Texas-Louisiana border. He used every trick in the book—and a number that weren't—every blandishment, every ounce of personal charm and charisma he could emote, to round up enough limited partnerships to enable him to make this great gamble. The stakes were huge: Make it and he'd be the wonder of the oil industry. Fail, and he'd be bankrupt and disgraced.

Hour after hour, with monotonous sameness, the diesel power plant kept generating the light to see and the power to sink the shaft deeper and deeper into the earth. According to the geological report, he had expected the moment of truth to occur at 870 feet. *Nothing but shale!* Another chance, according to his geologist, would be at 1,925 feet. *Nothing there but shale.* He had been there at the rig, day and night, so long that he had almost lost all track of time or reality: All that existed on this planet was this rig, this crew, this downward shaft.

Now, at almost dawn, the biting drill approached the last possible hope, at 2,742 feet. If this too proved dry, he'd be ruined. Suddenly, it hit, and a dark geyser shot high up into the heavens. The men shouted in exultation and did dances around the derrick. Charles could only stand there, numb with relief. *He'd made it!*

That proved an understatement, for the entire field turned out to be a veritable gold mine. Not satisfied with developing this bonanza, he'd gone on and on, working around the clock seven days a week, stopping only to eat a little and to catnap, in his mania to gain the mountaintop.

He sold out—at just the right time, it turned out—and invested in something his gut instinct told him might outperform oil—computers and software: Microsoft, Dell, Intel, and the Internet. He started with a small fortune and ended up a billionaire.

Now that he was awash in money, he quit work and dedicated the rest of his life to play, to sensation. He brought the same single-mindedness to his play he'd earlier given his work. He crisscrossed the planet as whim determined. Handsome, charismatic, and rich as King Croesus, the world thronged to his door. Unable to rid himself completely of his Christian upbringing, he refused to "experiment" with substance abuse, and thus he retained his health and stamina. His mountain-climbing exploits became legendary. He was the darling of the tabloids, always good for copy, and *People* magazine adored him.

While often in the company of beautiful women, none of the relationships lasted. None filled the void Sunny had left. Each one adorned his adventures for a while, like so much window dressing. Each was left wondering why he failed to return phone calls or to answer letters. A staff member had standing orders to toss these discarded women a few baubles as solace for the passing of his sun.

Having long loved the water and the many worlds of the Chesapeake Bay, he purchased one of the grandest estates in Maryland, on the Severn River. From this base, as the seasons passed, he ventured, he played, he lived for the moment, for the sensation. When *Forbes* listed him as one of America's richest, he had to tighten security because of the shysters who descended on him like clouds of locusts.

Now, in the darkest hours of this September night, at the conclusion of this audit of his life, he leaned back in his chair again, idly scratching Sylvester's silky head. Sylvester, his wants and desires met, purred. Charles, on the other hand, could see little reason to purr. He thought of an aphorism he had often repeated:

"What is the value of money, except for the happiness it brings?"

Now he dared to ask himself the ultimate questions: *Has money brought me happiness? Or has it brought me instead mere sensation? If I were truly happy, would I be so utterly bored with all life and limitless money have to offer?*

He knew the answers even as he articulated the questions. In all that truly mattered in life, he was bankrupt. He had no real friends. He had failed both as a son and as a brother. He had given up the only woman he had ever loved because of his bullheaded refusal to change course. He had in no way made the world a better place by giving away portions of his vast wealth to deserving causes. And—worst of all—he had treated God Himself with icy disdain.

Was it humanly possible to be a greater failure than this?

For the first time since boyhood, he felt shame. For the first time since boyhood, he felt remorse.

He wept.

Running Away to the Mountains

Once again, he ran away—fleeing to the mountains, this time, to have it out with his soul. As his Learjet began its long descent, ahead of him and his copilot loomed the vast bulwark of the Rockies—to the right, Long's and Meeker, Indian Peaks, and Never Summer Range; dead center, Mount Evans; and to his left that great landmark of westward-crossing pioneers, Pike's Peak, sere and bare in the late September sky.

His heart—could it be he still had one?—gave an unexpected leap as a hymn from his childhood emerged out of the mists of time: "Flee as a bird to the mountains." Might there be an answer for him in these majestic mountains?

After signing papers at the curb, he picked up a silver Jeep Cherokee with gray leather seats and threw two large gym bags into the back. One bag contained regulation clothes, the other hiking boots, two jackets (one lightweight and one heavy down), bottled water, and a sleeping bag.

About twenty minutes later, he was speeding westward toward the city known as the Queen of the Plains. Soon he drew up at Denver's venerable Brown Palace Hotel, a place that had grown on him with the passing of the years.

After dinner, he wandered down Sixteenth Street Mall to the new Barnes & Noble, determining not to leave until he had found what he sought: answers to life's three greatest questions:

Who am I?

Where have I come from?

Where am I going?

It was closing time before he had selected all the titles that interested him most. One of them was Sunny's new book.

Through the years, with alarming regularity and consistency, the face of Elizabeth had haunted him. Especially that last stricken, disbelieving look she had given him! There was no escape from it. Whether he was climbing Mount McKinley, fishing off Bora Bora, paddling down a Peruvian river, or stopping before a painting at the Louvre, at the strangest and most unexpected moments, *that look* would come back to him.

No, he had not been able to forget her. In fact, greatly to his chagrin, he found himself keeping tabs on her. He knew when she graduated from college, when she got her master's, and when she got her Ph.D. He even knew where she taught. He was intrigued by the growing national recognition of her writing 'stature. Prose first, and now poetry.

Elizabeth Emma Bond. Yes, her very name still moved him, brought a catch to his throat, and a sigh at all that he had lost. He wondered if she had ever married—so many married women retained their maiden names for professional reasons these days. He wondered if she had ever really loved anyone else.

Next morning early, he was in the Cherokee, heading up the long incline to Eisenhower Tunnel. Later in the day, he turned north off Interstate 70 at Rifle; at Meeker, he swung east. Later, as the pavement ran out, he continued on, up, up, and up a dirt road winding through aspen groves ablaze with green, gold, and mandarin orange. At last, ahead of him he saw the lodge and rather primitive-looking cabins. The one closest to the singing White River was reserved for him.

After dinner in the lodge, he walked out under the aspens and spruce and drank in the nighttime sounds of the forest. It was cold: fall was in the air. He built a fire in his cabin stove before he climbed into bed. For once he had no trouble sleeping, for the river sang him a lullaby.

The next morning he got up in time to watch the sun come up over Trappers Lake. It almost took his breath away as first the rim turned crimson and gold, and then the fiery stain plunged downward to the brownish lakes and river; soon Trappers Lake turned green, then light blue, then deep blue, highlighted by the flaming aspens. Towering thousands of feet above were the great monolithic mesas, already dusted with snow. Taken all together, arguably one of the loveliest scenes in all the great West, one deeply loved by America's greatest western frontier writer, Zane Grey. Something softened inside Charles, for—overwhelmed by the beauty of the scene—he found himself, unaccountably, struggling to hold back the tears. All around him he heard the twittering and cawing of the birds. Iridescent ducks landed and took off from the lake, shattering its mirror smoothness. From not far away, but out of sight, he heard the *thwack* sound of a beaver tail. And out in the middle of the lake two fishermen in a bright red canoe seemed suspended in space.

Finally, he tore himself away from the ever-changing scene and returned to the lodge for breakfast. After that, he could delay no longer the reckoning: the search for answers.

In his knapsack that first day lay only one book, C. S. Lewis's *Mere Christianity*. He had first heard about the book when still in college but was then both uninterested in it and unready for it—now he was. Halfway around the lake, he sat down, leaned back on a large rock, and opened the deceptively small volume. He soon discovered what millions before him already knew: It is anything but small inside! Some of the heaviest thoughts ever articulated lined up in neat rows on those few pages.

He read slowly, challenging Lewis to prove his points. So long had Charles been away from God that he felt it necessary to seek out an intermediary; he didn't dare seek God out on his own. Not after all the years of insolence and neglect.

The second day, he read it again, only this time he stopped every few pages in order to write down his thoughts and responses in the large journal he had purchased in Denver. The third day, he read it again. By this time, in his mind, he had admitted that God indeed existed. Now came the time to read the Bible, starting with the New Testament.

Day followed day, and week followed week, chapter followed chapter. Charles lost himself in the word pictures of those who had been with Christ in the wedding at Cana, in the boat during the storm, on a hillside with the five thousand, with the Samaritan woman at a well, with a repentant Mary Magdalene kneeling at His feet. Especially was he jolted by the story of the rich young ruler and Christ's injunction to go and sell all that he had and give to the poor.

Then he left the stories of Jesus for a time as he immersed himself in scriptural biography. He had never before realized how painfully honest these portraits really were! He couldn't help identifying with Solomon, who *had* everything, who *knew* everything, and who ultimately was bored by it all. Other books by or about great men and women of faith he studied, alternating them with his study of the Bible.

All this took place against the backdrop of the aspens, as their colors grew more intense; then, no longer able to hold on, the leaves began to let go, one by one floating lazily down to the forest floor. Indian Summer wandered in and showed no signs of wanting to leave.

Again Charles returned to the New Testament. He fell in love with God the Son in the Gospels, as the ministry of Jesus on earth opened gradually to his understanding. From them, and from the apostle Paul, he gained fresh insights into the new life Christ offered him through His life, death, and resurrection.

One day in late October, he climbed the great Chinese Wall, on the western side of the valley, all the way to the top. There he sat down on its edge, drinking in the paradise below. Then it hit him: *Life without God is not life at all, but merely an existence. No wonder I was bored. Only Life can beget life! Only God can fill a man with something greater than self.* Self, he now knew, from studying Solomon and others, was corrosive and terribly destructive, as evil as the pride that spawns it. The thought drove him to his knees.

He raised his eyes up into and through that deep blue Colorado sky, and prayed his first prayer since boyhood:

"Lord, I know I'm nothing without You—less than nothing. So far in my life, it's been all take and no give. But now, whatever I have, whatever I am—precious little though it be—I give to You to do with as You will."

Instantly, there swept through him sensations new to him. Energy flooded into his brain, soul, and heart. *Yes!* Oh, a thousand times yes! *He had a heart!* At last, at long last, he could read that wrenching book of poetry, written by Sunny, without dying inside when he read those lines describing the man he'd been (or at least he *assumed* they referred to him).

It was one of the earliest poems in the collection, titled "The Hollow Man."

> Oh he was handsome, beautiful as a Greek god,
> But he was empty: a hollow boom-booming drum;
> Oh he could speak, could sway multitudes,
> But inside, where his heart should have been,
> There was only sawdust, straw,
> And swirling, mocking winds.

He soon discovered that she had both gained and lost in the years since he had known her; gained greatly in stature, in maturity, in wisdom; lost somewhat in that hers was a darker world-view than it once had been. And he winced when he remembered his role in that process.

One late afternoon as the shadows began to climb the ramparts, he stopped by a brook at the far side of the valley floor, found a comfortable place in which to think and dream, and without any conscious volition, his thoughts again swung back to that very real connection between Sunny and God in his life story. He could not think very long about either one without also thinking about the other.

He pulled out of his knapsack his already-worn copy of Elizabeth's *Songs in the Night*. Third on the *New York Times* bestsellers list. Somehow he could not seem to get enough of her and her spiritual odyssey. He searched her poems with all the intensity of a detective hot on a gradually warming criminal trail. Even so, gradually, the photographic image of what she had become came into focus in the darkroom tray of his mind. Crucial to this process was a section in her introduction that fascinated him. He had marked it and underlined it, so it was easy to find:

When God created us, He deliberately fashioned an expandable or contractable cavern deep in the psyche, the core of our beings, the inviolate inner sanctum of our selfhood that no one ever sees, not even ourselves. Dwelling in this space are three highly individualistic personhoods: the Mind, the Heart, and the Soul. And a fourth—God. Only God can keep the other three from destroying themselves and each other, for only He outranks them.

In fact, without God this chamber becomes a hellhole, awash with internecine blood. None of the three can survive living in that chamber without God. It becomes a void because it cannot be filled without God's presence.

The battling trio sometimes tries all kinds of substitutes for God, hauling in off the streets such diverse friends as Greed, Lust, Envy, Wealth, Pride, License, Vanity, Narcissus, Self-Gratification, Substance Abuse, Cruelty, Selfishness, Ambition, Intellectualism, Idleness, Sloth, Ignorance—oh, their names are legion! Suffice it to say that the carnage is awful! None of them can survive that chamber for more than minutes at a time.

Not even "good" friends like Agape, Truth, Integrity, Humility, Generosity, Work, Kindness,

Growth, and Health can survive this chamber
long without God in it. Inevitably, they end up
distorting their positive qualities and thus must
flee to save themselves.

Ultimately, without God's sanctifying and
blessing presence, it is safe to say that the owner
of that unfillable void has no mind, no soul, and
no heart, for all three have fled who knows where,
and will never return to that cavern to stay—
unless God is there to protect them from each
other.

But when God is invited in and made to feel
welcome, from that moment on, the contraction
ceases and the cavern begins to expand as the
three erstwhile enemies begin to live at peace with
each other and grow into the giants each is capable
of becoming. Otherwise, each would continue to
shrink into dwarfhood.

"Alas!" sighed Charles. "She speaks the truth! That's
why she called me a 'hollow man'—I *was* hollow, for neither my Heart nor my Soul could function without God's
presence within me. Only my Mind, and without God to
guide him, he is self-destructive, even suicidal."

Oh, Sunny! Sunny! You've moved on so far beyond me during the years since I last saw you. I wonder if the distance can ever be bridged?

At the top of one day's agenda was the writing of letters, chief of which were the long catching-up-with-the-years ones he wrote to his folks, brother, and sister. In each one he detailed his journey, his finding God, and his desire to be reunited with his family.

Those done, he turned to the most difficult letter of all—Sunny's! What could he say—what should he say to her that would cause her to answer back? Whatever she knew of him would certainly not prejudice her in his favor. Finally, he decided to keep the letter light and briefly bridge across the story of the years, but close with three serious paragraphs. He wrestled hours over them before he was satisfied:

I am here at Trappers Lake for my health—spiritual health. After all the long years, I have come back to God. I am at peace for the first time since I can remember.

Especially can I relate to the passage in your new book, on page 11, that refers to that cavern within us that is unfillable without God. I know that's true for I've tried to fill it again and again, with every possible kind of substitute. None of them worked.

Now I am facing the rest of my life with new courage and new joy. But also sadness, because of the needless pain I have inflicted on those who mean the most to me. Never have I been able to forget the cruelty of my last words to you! You have every right to never speak or write to me again. But I am banking on your inherent kindness and forgiving nature, that you will drop me a line and let me know how things are going with you.

I can be reached at P.O. Box 600, Arnold, Maryland 20202, in about a week.

> Very sincerely yours,
> Charlie

Then he sealed it, with a sigh and a prayer, and mailed it to her, in care of her publisher.

During his last week in the Flattops, he hiked up to emerald green Little Trappers Lake every morning, planning out the rest of his life. What should he do with it? More specifically, what was he going to do with his billions? Several things he'd already settled for sure: Life without work was dead-end and devoid of either meaning or happiness. The same was true of a life devoted to accumulating rather than giving. Furthermore, a life lived at variance to a positive moral code sooner or later short-circuits and blows out one's emotional and nervous system.

His spiritual life in order, his goal-setting all but complete, he now knew his mountain sabbatical was over. He had found the meaning in life that had so long eluded him.

At last he could delay his departure no longer: Day after tomorrow he'd return to the demands of civilization. With this one last day, he decided he'd climb 12,246-foot-high Sheep Mountain, three thousand feet above the valley floor. The day began with a cloudless sky, but by the time he got to the top, clouds began to roll in. The temperature began to drop—and then plunged. Indian Summer gave way to lazy snowflakes, seemingly in no hurry to get anywhere. Then, within mere minutes, the snow intensified: snowflakes growing fatter and fatter and falling faster and faster. It offered a once-in-a-lifetime vista: watching the snow fall from such a height!

Reluctantly, Charles left his aerie and headed down the ramparts to the valley so far below. He lost his way again and again. Visibility became almost nonexistent, and he now had a full-fledged blizzard to deal with. The wind was beginning to howl. At one point of near panic, when he felt completely lost, he prayed, "Lord, You know I've surrendered my life to You. If You feel there is more work for me to do here on earth, please guide me safely down." Immediately, panic and disorientation left him, and he felt a sense of peace and safety. Then the blizzard slowed just long enough for him to find the trail again. It was night when he stumbled into the lodge, snow encrusted and half frozen. The lodge manager had almost given up hope of ever seeing him alive again.

By now the winds shrieked with near hurricane strength. All that night, all the next day, all the next night and day, the storm raged on. Finally, three days after it struck, the storm ebbed, leaving in its wake a record nine feet of newly fallen snow. When the sun finally came out again, he looked out from the lodge (where both guests and employees had come for safety, warmth, and food) at a pristine new world. A hymn, long forgotten, reassured him: "Whiter Than Snow." His soul felt as clean and white as the snow that blinded him outside the window.

Over a week went by before the road could be reopened. Thus it was mid-November before he at last arrived home. In the mail—oh joy of joys!—was a letter from Sunny. Like his own, it was light and noncommittal, but it opened a door nonetheless. He answered it that very day. Soon letters flew back and forth once a week. In one of hers came the long-awaited question: "By what values do you live today?" He spent a lot of time on his answer.

ANOTHER EASTER

Since returning to Maryland, Charles had studied the lives and philosophies of great givers such as George Peabody, Andrew Carnegie, John D. Rockefeller, Andrew Mellon, William Hewlett, and J. C. Penney, not just to learn about the scope of their giving but, more important, the reasons they gave. He was fascinated by J. C. Penney's contention that it was virtually impossible to outgive God: *The higher the percentage given away, the greater the return on what was left!* He read with equal fascination Henry Van Dyke's *The Mansion* and Lloyd C. Douglas's *The Magnificent Obsession* to study such selfless giving as expressed in fiction.

He also studied The Foundation Center's listing of top U.S. foundations and what causes each supported. Some he had heard of before; others were new to him. University foundations such as those run by Harvard, Duke, Texas, and Yale, he paid little attention to, for their goals would be different from his. Rather, he spent a great deal of time scrutinizing the great foundation powerhouses, such as Lilly,

Ford, Packard, Kellogg, Getty, Johnson, Pew, MacArthur, Woodruff, Rockefeller, Mellon, Starr, and Kresge. He and his staff also spent a lot of time on the phone with directors of these foundations. He had no wish to merely clone what others were doing; rather, he earnestly desired to plow new ground.

It was February before he and his team of CPAs, researchers, and attorneys completed their assignments. It was time to put all the pieces together. Heading his team was his personal attorney, John, a partner in one of the world's largest law firms. Up until recent months, he and Charles had never been close, the relationship all business. But that had changed by the time that long-awaited day arrived, when Charles called the top leaders of the team together for final reports. Outside, the Severn was still frozen clear across to the other side, a mile away, and snow was falling.

It took all day for all the reports to be given. In fact, it was evening before it was complete, and late evening before the celebratory dinner was over and things were restored to normal by the chef and kitchen crew. One by one his associates left, until at last only Charles and John were left. A fire roared in the great fireplace, and Sylvester yawned contentedly in his lap.

John, tired but clearly excited, finally leaned forward and said, "Well, Charles, it's been *quite* a day!"

Charles nodded.

"Are we where you wanted to be?"

"Yes, I cannot think of anything we forgot."

John grinned a bit wearily in tacit agreement.

"Well, John, I guess the moment of truth has come at last. I'm…uh…I'm ready to *do* it."

"I thought so."

"Yes, most of my assets will go into the foundation. I guess the key question now is, What is my current net worth? I didn't want to ask that question while the others were here."

"I understand."

"Now, I know it's not easy for you to answer me, because so many of my investments are nonliquid."

"That's true, but I can still get pretty close."

"That's good enough for me."

"All right," and here John pulled out a leather binder and opened it to a well-marked page. "Let's see…stocks, bonds, municipals, mutuals, the whole gamut, comes to about eleven billion and a quarter. Uh…property is valued (conservatively) at around two and three quarters…miscellaneous about one and a half…and the cash and quickly liquid—seven hundred fifty mil. Of course, taxes haven't been paid yet this year."

"But what I turn over to the foundation isn't going to be hurt much by the IRS."

"That's true. Let me check this on my trusty ol' calculator. Looks like, all together, there's a little over sixteen billion…How much of that would you like to see transferred across? *Eventually,* of course. This is going to take a *lot* of time. Probably a year or two before it's all complete."

"*All* of it—except for the liquid stuff."

"*What?* Did I hear you correctly?"

"You did. And even so, much that I am retaining will probably end up in the foundation before I'm through."

"Do you realize that you are talking about a foundation with assets rivaling those of Lilly, Ford, and Packard? It would be one of the world's largest! And you also realize that such a massive transfer is irreversible?"

"I do." He paused, a pensive look in his eyes. "Yes. With the Lord's help—and yours—I'd like to do it. I'd like to make a real difference in this sad ol' world before I'm through."

"All right, it can be done—with one condition."

"What's that?"

"Can I be on the board—*pro bono?*"

"Only on that basis?"

"*Only.*"

"*Done!* Now, let's make it happen."

…"Say, Charles, I've got one more favor to ask of you."

"Shoot."

"Would you mind—just to settle my curiosity—telling me what *really* happened to you at Trappers Lake?"

"Not at all," and here a faraway look came to Charles's eyes. "John, you are perhaps aware that I haven't been the nicest person to know."

His companion said nothing, but his lips twitched with just a flicker of a smile.

"For about as far back as I can remember, I have lived only for myself and the fortune I planned to amass. I didn't care what I had to do, or whom I had to hurt, in the process. I was a machine without a heart…In fact"—and here he paused, his face momentarily etched with pain—"a long time ago the only woman I ever loved declared me to be a 'hollow man.'"

"I've been wondering if perhaps there wasn't a woman somewhere behind all this. There often is, you know."

"Yes, and here's proof of how high my stock is with her today. By the way, she's become famous and a best-selling author. You might have heard of her." Here he handed John the volume, indicating a certain well-read page. "In her latest book is a poem you'll find more than a little interesting. Read 'The Hollow Man!'"

John read silently for a few minutes, then rested the book on his lap. "Phew! She doesn't mince words, does she? Come to think of it, I've heard this book is really making waves. My sister saw the author interviewed by Barbara Walters—was quite impressed. Any thoughts of reestablishing contact with her?"

"I already have."

"Oh?"

"Yes, I already have, and we are corresponding. She doesn't yet know about all this."

"Oh."

"But she will, in due time."

"But—there *has* to be more to it than that."

"There is. Oh, there *is!* Let's see…How can I best express it? John, out there on the Flattop Mountains—I found God. In fact, my life was totally changed there."

"How so?"

"By reading about, studying, and reflecting on Christ's life, death, and resurrection—that's what *really* happened."

It was Easter Sunday in Nashville. The sun was shining and the greens were so vibrant they seemed unreal. For weeks now, Nature's brush had been painting the South, brushing on a new coat of primroses, hyacinths, daffodils, tulips, azaleas, and dogwoods. Inside the great cathedral, the faithful were gathering in attire rivaling the colors outside. The organ's thunder shook the earth, sending chills up one's spine, with Charles Wesley's triumphant hymn, "Christ the Lord Is Risen Today." Along the outside aisles next to the stained-glass windows and massed at the front were hundreds of Easter lilies, their fragrance engulfing the congregation.

Attracting little notice in the vast crowd, a tall good-looking man in a suit of muted gray was ushered down the central aisle to a bench in the front section. No one watching his calm demeanor would have guessed that his heart was shuddering, both with Easter joy and with suspense generated by a woman he had not seen in twenty-three long years. Was it still over, or could it be there was still a chance for him?

The usher stopped, turned around, and motioned to his left. And *there* was Sunny, dressed in emerald green, a vision of springtime herself. Even though they had caught up with the years in their letters, even though there appeared to be a meeting of hearts, souls, and minds on paper, there still remained that ultimate test: *Would that intangible that we glibly label* love *still be there?* Without it, friendship was all there could ever be. She smiled tremulously as her eyes drank in the sight of him. He, on the other hand, could not have even told her his name, had she asked. All he could think of was the possibility of the impossible—and the radiant reality of her presence next to him.

They had little time to speak to each other, for the service was already beginning. In it, the Good News of Christ's birth, life, death, and resurrection was told once again, both in word and in music. And now the congregation had risen to sing those life-changing words, "I serve a risen Savior, He's in the world today."

Once, while holding the hymnal, their hands touched, and it was as if an electric shock arced between them. Each concluded that the years had dealt gently with the other. Far more significantly, however, she had searched for sham, pride, or subterfuge, but found none. Instead, he radiated a new seriousness, earnestness, and reverence for God that she'd never observed in him before. Clearly, God was now the most important thing in life to him, more central to his being than even she could ever be.

As the hymn came to an end, Charles closed his eyes and silently prayed his first Easter prayer of dedication.

Now that he was once again clean inside, he dared to ask his Lord—if it might be His will—to bless the great love he still felt for Elizabeth. For Sunny!

As he opened his eyes, he saw that she had been watching him, and on her lovely face was a glow that was not all Easter. In her eyes he read tenderness, trust, admiration, and joy.

And promise.